THE BALANCING ACT

Getting and Keeping Your Life in Balance

Paul Heneks

FRASER PUBLISHING COMPANY
Burlington, Vermont

Published by Fraser Publishing Company
a division of
Fraser Management Associates, Inc.
Box 494
Burlington, Vermont 05402

Library of Congress Catalog Card Number: 94-61885
ISBN: 0-87034-119-7

Cover Design: Susan Heneks
Cover Photo: Carl Clark

Printed in the United States of America
♻ *Text printed on recycled paper.*

To Susan:

*The brightest star, the most beautiful
rose, and the greatest joy of my life.*

Contents

Chapter Seven 135
The Best Is Yet to Come

Notes 143

Index 151

About the Author 159

Author's Note

The Balancing Act focuses on posturing oneself for success by learning to balance your health, finances, relationships, and the environment. How we share this planet with a reverence for each other enables all of us to grow toward a happy, healthy, and productive life.

Realizing all of these subjects have been written about before, I had to ask myself, what makes this book different? Dolly Parton wrote the song "I Will Always Love You" twenty-two years ago, but its greatest success did not come until after it was sung by Whitney Houston in the movie soundtrack "The Bodyguard." It's all in the timing and delivery.

The extremists in life are usually very gifted, talented people who bring focus or attention to change. While that is true, it is also my experience that extremes often do not keep the attention of everyone else. The key to all of this is balance, and without it we are always just a little left or right of center. It is my hope that after reading this you are encouraged, enlightened, and motivated to move forward in the spirit of finding your balance, and recognizing that change creates opportunity.

Acknowledgments

We are a reflection of all our relationships and experiences. It is only with the help of others that we obtain the present. I would like to thank several people who have been a presence in my life through their support, direction, friendship, and love.

To my brother-in-law, Pat McDevitt, who is always there for a great workout. To my CPA Gary Kushner, who has always been a loyal friend. To Kent Mangelson, the best mutual fund wholesaler I have ever known, for his contribution to chapters two and three. To Pam Dils for her help in coordinating the compliance of chapter four. To Dr. John Cotant, for reviewing chapter five, during what I know is a busy schedule as a father of nine and a cardiologist. To registered dietitian, Wendy Schwartz, for her comments and suggestions. To Yvonne Johns, for both her editorial and organizational help.

To Phil Carret, ninety-seven years young, one of the wisest men in the investment field, who taught me the contrarian view of the market and has been an inspiration since the day we met twenty-three years ago.

To all the animals who have brought so much laughter and joy to my life, and taught me the meaning of unconditional love and that all too fading quality of loyalty. I thank and miss them all.

Finally, to my wife Susan, whom I have had the pleasure of sharing the past twenty-six years as best friend, constant companion, loyal supporter, and the greatest joy any person could ever hope or dream of sharing their life. Her efforts on this project have enabled me to bring a ten-year goal to its conclusion.

Introduction

Who better to write about the author than his companion of 26 years, his wife Susan.

Paul grew up in a working class neighborhood of Detroit. Due to an undetected reading disorder as a young child, he struggled through school. A college professor told him that he would either be a failure or a millionaire by the age of thirty.

After serving as an infantryman in the Vietnam War, he began his business career at the age of twenty-three. He always wrote down his goals, and said "It's not enough to have them in your head, you have to put them on paper, accept the challenge and never lose sight of your dream." Paul focused on how to achieve each goal, and by the age of thirty had made his first million.

All of this came at a price. Paul's passion for work began to affect his health and peace of mind. He realized that his life was not in balance.

Now the *goal* was obvious. The *challenge* before him; to somehow balance a working life without sacrificing a personal *dream*.

I hope this book will inspire you to set your own goals, strive for your most daring dreams and, most of all, find that precious balance.

This was written with unending gratitude for sharing his life, his love and his wonderful dreams with me.

Chapter One

Recognizing a Need for Change

Prosperous careers, marriages, parenthood, and philanthropic endeavors are just a few ways success is measured. One of the most distinctive characteristics of success is balance. To achieve balance, you must learn to manage that which creates your state of mind: health, relationships, and finances. Any aspect of your life that becomes extremely unbalanced will cause unfortunate emotional and physical consequences. This can result in poor health, divorce, and financial ruin. Environmental imbalance leads to ecological disaster. Lack of communication harbors hostility, anger, and resentment. The consequences of imbalance, in any of these areas, can lead to unhappiness and disruption of lifestyle. Good or bad habits and behavior have a tendency to continue. Changing our behavior enables us to enjoy a healthy, happy, and a more productive life.

The focus is to first establish a foundation of financial success in order to set the stage to balance other areas of your life. This chapter explains why today a growing number of the working class and retirees are being deprived of the American dream and how this can be changed. We will identify ways to produce income, accumulate, and maintain wealth. To better understand success in this context, we must first define wealth.

Wealth is the accumulation of assets resulting in financial independence. Money is simply a commodity with no intrinsic value—other than what it can buy. Money can buy financial freedom and allows you to do what you want, when you want, and with whom you want.

"Subtract a person's material wealth and
what is left is his real wealth."
—Malcolm S. Forbes, Sr.

There are more than ninety-six million households in the United States, yet only about 3 percent have a net worth of over $600,000. Only 1.5 percent of these households has a net worth of more than $1,000,000. The top 20 percent of all wage earners in this country earn 80 percent of the income. The average American millionaire is self-employed and owns a business. Only 16 percent of millionaires work for someone else.

Hypothetically, if you divided all the assets of this country equally among everyone, in time, the original wealthy people would accumulate it again. We know that successful people have very definite habits. So the questions become: What are these habits and how do we develop the habits for achieving financial success and become one of these individuals? Money does not create happiness, but it sure makes life easier—and a lot more fun!

Categories of People

Other than individuals living below the poverty line of $14,335 for a family of four, there are essentially three categories of people: the rich, the wealthy, and the wanna-be's.

The *rich* differ from the others because they have capital working for them. They may no longer have to work for themselves, a luxury they achieved through the accumulation of assets. In many cases, this group is unidentifiable because they often go to great lengths to look mainstream.

The second group, the *wealthy,* have attained a comfortable lifestyle. They may enjoy the benefits associated with their achievements, e.g., travel, beautiful homes, automobiles, and private schools; however, they must continue to generate income to maintain that position. They have not accumulated sufficient assets to continue their lifestyle without earned income. Conversely, they usually go to great lengths to appear rich.

The third group, the *wanna-be's*, experience a great deal of financial pressure and stress. They live from paycheck to paycheck, often beyond their means. Most of their lifestyle, if not all, is financed in one way or another. They want to drive the right car, live in the right neighborhood, belong to the right club, etc. Most are over-leveraged and unprepared for any life contingency that may destroy their standard of living at any time. On the surface, they keep up an appearance of doing well with little financial basis.

> *"Money seldom changes people, it just*
> *makes them more visible."*
> —Malcolm S. Forbes, Sr.

What sets the financially successful apart from everyone else? Successful people have developed the habit of first visualizing a dream before it can be achieved. Consider the story of an automobile salesman who coached prospective buyers to drive the car alongside a shiny glass window. This approach showed them how the car made them look in the reflection. Once they saw themselves this way, and realized how others would see them, it helped close the sale.

There is a common denominator among successful people. The affluent are willing to share their experience and knowledge with anyone interested. They embrace the attitude that they will continue to grow and further their careers regardless of the competition. The people from whom it is most difficult to obtain information are those in the less successful category. This group considers information to be proprietary in nature and are reluctant to share it with their contemporaries. Their concern is that someone might catch up or pass them.

Government vs Business

Why then, does the general public often view the wealthy with such disdain? The popularity of the lottery and sweepstakes would suggest that most people would prefer to be wealthy. Yet, it is the wealthy who generally take the greatest risks, generate the most capital, pay the most taxes (contrary to popular opinion), and create the most jobs. The government raises taxes, subsequently burdening everyone, but the wealthy are most often the target. The government defines wealth as any household making $50,000 or more per year. The median income of married families in 1992 was $42,064, meaning half of all households have incomes above this amount and half below. That's not so wealthy anymore when to make ends meet, the majority of households require two working spouses. The average working person and retiree in this country today is being taxed right out of the American dream.

The 1993 tax increase takes the top tax rate to 39.6 percent. When you factor in your state tax, social security tax, and several phased-out deductions, the effective rate is closer to 50 percent. This does not include payroll tax, sales tax, use tax, excise tax, business tax, property tax, and personal property tax, just to name a few. In fact, personal exemptions have been shrinking. The median income for a family of four in 1954 was $4,233 with exemptions of $2,400 equaling 56.7 percent of income. In 1994 the same family of four with a median income of $38,000 only has exemptions of $9,400 or 24.7 percent of income. When Americans deplete their savings or businesses reduce investments to pay higher taxes, U.S. economic activity is adversely affected.

A case in point is the recent 10 percent luxury tax repealed in August of 1993 on boats and aircraft. A report for the Congressional Joint Committee on taxation in 1991 predicted the boat tax would raise $3 million that fiscal year but cost the government $18.2 million in lost revenue and unemployment costs. Just one example: Hatteras yachts in High Point, N.C., cut 700 of 1,700 jobs from 1988 to 1992. During the same period, the marine division's revenue sank nearly 25 percent to $1.5 billion, laid off 8000 workers, and closed sixteen plants. The past year since the 10 percent luxury tax has been repealed, 1,500 positions have been refilled. There are similar stories in the aircraft industry. Instead of taxing the rich for their toys, it just put people out of work. Consequently, the government realized this only after nearly destroying several industries. The luxury tax had exactly the opposite effect on revenue as intended. It didn't take a rocket scientist to figure this out in the first place, but it was one more political attempt to make the wealthy the bad guys. Higher taxes stop growth and cause unemployment. Lower taxes create growth and jobs, therefore generating more tax revenue to the government from the wages of more employed workers.

Another example of partisan politics is when the capital gains tax (always argued as a tax benefit for the rich) is lowered. It creates economic stimulus by providing the incentive to buy and sell stocks, bonds, real estate, and other investments, which in turn generates taxable gains, providing higher tax revenue and capital creation, to the government and investors. Historically, when tax rates are reduced, as they were in 1981 by President Reagan, the wealthy segment of the economy stimulates business by the creation of capital through expansion, research, and development. This fosters higher wages and growth, all of which generates more taxes. This, in turn, reduces borrowing, lowers interest costs, and eases inflationary pressure, providing more capital at lower rates. The end result is a more productive and stronger society and economy. As taxes increase, businesses become more defensive by positioning themselves to hire fewer people, spend less money, and build fewer plants. This, consequently, creates less capital and a lower tax base. The economy stagnates, causing higher unemployment, less consumer spending, and higher debts. This results in creating a higher demand on borrowing, rising interest rates, and inflation that erodes purchasing power and lowers the standard of living. The domino effect continues, and causes greater dependence on welfare and entitlement programs. This forces the government to raise taxes to pay for these programs. This vicious cycle perpetuates itself in loss of hope, self-esteem, desperation, and deterioration of our economic base. The problem is that few people or politicians have sufficient leadership to pay the price of change until a crisis forces us to change.

The government should be equally accountable to balance the budget no differently than any individual or company who goes out of business if they fail to balance their own budget. If the government spends more than they collect in revenue, they either devalue the dollar by printing more money (which compromises future purchasing power) or raise our taxes, a luxury the taxpayers or businesses do not have. Taxpayers don't mind paying their fair share, so long as the government would be more responsible in cutting unnecessary and wasteful expenses. According to a recent poll published in *Time*, people today trust the government to do what's right, always or most of the time, only 19 percent of the time compared to 76 percent in 1964.

I have never understood why this mentality of raising taxes is so pervasive in government, while they, in turn, do little to responsibly cut government spending and deal with these issues. President Clinton's 1993 tax increase defers cost-cutting measures to the future, while the tax increase was retroactive to the beginning of 1993. This was such a blatant tax increase so late in the year that taxpayers were given the ability to pay the difference between the prior and the new tax liability over the next three years with no interest, providing little consolation to frustrated taxpayers.

Getting Re-elected

One problem with our system today is that politicians spend a great deal of time and money in the last two years of their term preparing to get re-elected. President Nixon's 1970 salary of $200,000, adjusted for inflation, would be $773,380 in today's dollars. President Clinton's $200,000 salary on the same inflation- adjusted basis makes him the lowest paid president in history (If President Clinton is a one-term president). The average term of all forty-two presidents who served in office has been five years. An answer to this problem may be a one-term presidency of six years with a salary of $1,000,000; thus, attracting business oriented individuals to office.

The world of politics is changing. Rather than more taxes, more spending, and more government, we could use less government and fewer politicians held to higher standards to formulate the more complex issues for voters to decide. According to a recent survey, 76 percent of Americans favor a national referendum system in which all citizens vote on all proposals that deal with major national issues. If the American voters approved a project, it would be the administration's responsibility to carry it out regardless of party politics. As an example, how many times and for what purposes will the space shuttle be launched at the taxpayers expense of $500 million dollars or the building of the $8.3 billion super-conducting super collider, only to be shelved by the next administration?

The list is endless, but other areas that need desperate reform that would ease the need to continue raising taxes are the liability, litigation, and welfare system. The welfare system was originally intended to provide assistance to the widowed, blind, and disabled. Today those abusing the system provide a disincentive to work and make a mockery of the program. The court system, clogged with nuisance and frivolous law suits, is costing the taxpayers an immeasurable amount of money. We are becoming a nation of victims who encourage law suits and are increasingly not accountable for our actions. This trend will permanently cripple, if not destroy, the American dream. These governmental policies, slow to change, will force you to either lower your standard of living or earn more. To maintain or increase our standard of living we must understand that to be successful in business it is important you achieve a certain level of competence we will call *professional status*.

The President and the Physician

In twenty-three years as a career broker, I have watched many salespeople try to understand why some of their peers succeeded while others struggled and failed. In the decades of Procter and Gamble's research into marketing soap, toothpaste and laundry detergent, I have found the answer to this question. The basis of the Procter and Gamble research defines the difference between selling and marketing. *Selling* is trying to make a product or service fit a client's needs in the best interest of the salesman. *Marketing*, on the other hand, attempts to satisfy the needs and best interests of the client. Marketing offers problems to solve—not products to sell. This research relates to all types of businesses and individuals offering a product or service, which brings us to the conclusion that we, in some form or another are all in sales.

Approximately one in six U.S. business people have a position defined as sales or marketing. The president of the United States, for example, attempts to sell an economic program to Congress. A physician offers his or her experience and confidence when performing a procedure. Even secretaries market their skills and achievements when they request a raise.

The word *salesman* often carries a negative connotation. There are good and bad in all professions: there are reputable and disreputable brokers, CPAs, attorneys, politicians, electricians, and doctors. In the negative, all of these could be described as salesmen, less than professional. Perception is often a greater factor than reality. Saddam Hussein's invasion of Kuwait conjured up apocalyptic scenarios in 1991, until U.S. and Coalition forces ended his reign of terror. Reading a book is often better than seeing the movie because our imagination can be greater than a director's ability to portray the story on the big screen.

World War II's most notorious German U-boat commander (Krutchmire) sank more Allied ships than anyone. The reason for his success was positioning. Instead of attacking the heavily armed perimeter of a convoy, he would navigate inside the destroyers and strategically take out unarmed cargo and troop ships. One of the strategies that finally crippled Hitler's war machine was the Allied forces' successful bombing of the German ball bearing factories. This slowed the completion of tank production: no ball bearings, no tanks. Whether you are positioning yourself on the battle field or in business, the strategy remains the same: to separate yourself. *Posturing* is not what you do with a product or service, it is what you do to the client's perception.

Your Next Client

A common denominator affecting whether you are perceived as a professional or as a salesmen is how you meet your prospect. For anyone in the service industry, the question most asked during a presentation is: "How much do you charge?" This question means your prospect has perceived you as a professional with value. What has transpired that you should be asked this question? Salesmen lacking professional status are usually not asked how much they charge. If you receive a referral from someone who does not regard you as a professional, the person referred will perceive you as less than professional (salesman). Likewise, if you receive a referral from a person who views you as a professional, your referral will perceive you as a professional.

There are a variety of ways to achieve professional status. The two most prominent methods are through referrals and seminars. Position yourself to approach a person you know, who may know another person, and ask them: "Will you tell your friend/colleague/relative about me?" Then when you call that prospective client, he or she has already heard of you.

I have dealt with prospects that are not referrals by requesting an informational interview, completing an analysis, and presenting a proposal. In some cases, the reason the prospect may procrastinate, "think about it," or take your idea and buy from someone who they view as a professional is because your introduction didn't come from a respected person.

It has also been my experience that quite the opposite happens when receiving an introduction from a respected person like an attorney or CPA. The reason I was perceived as a professional, rather than a salesman, was due to the credibility of the referring individual, and, normally, the prospect followed through with the recommendation.

CLIENT DEVELOPMENT LADDER

- Referral from personal friend or associate
- Referral from a professional (banker, CPA, attorney, doctor)

HIGH
CREDIBILITY

LOW
CREDIBILITY

- Meet at a lecture, lunch or dinner meeting as a group member
- Meet through a common interest (charity, club etc.)
- Attend seminar offered by salesperson in their office
- Telephone follow-up by salesperson responding to request for information
- Receive information in the mail
- See an advertisement in the local paper
- Receive a telephone call from a salesperson you've never met

Successful people learn how to achieve professional status and to compete well; if they do one of these well, they may be okay. For those who cannot do either one well, it is only a matter of time until they fail.

An example of using our time and resources ineffectively is demonstrated in America's junk mail mania. Research shows executives are prospected per week on the average of two-and-a-half times and receive more than 100 pieces of junk mail. Fifty pieces of mail are screened by their staff and discarded unopened. Twenty-five others are opened to determine if there is a check inside and then discarded. Of the remaining twenty-five, fifteen are examined for eight seconds or less, then thrown away. Only ten of these may be perused for eight seconds or more, to be filed, followed up, or purchased.

Most people in any sales position have been stood up for an appointment; I now understand why. When you are stood up, your prospective clients feel it is not important to keep the appointment and make the decision not to show. At the very least, they do not extend the professional courtesy of rescheduling or canceling. This is because you are not perceived as a professional, but as a salesman. A colleague of mine from the early years of my career was often stood up by a prospective client. When this happened, he would leave his business card in the door with a note on the back reading: "I was here, you were not, could it be you forgot?" Though it may be humorous today, it wasn't then.

Are You Losing Respect?

A recent survey judged the professional status of various industries. It found only 10 percent of the people polled gave the brokerage industry any degree of credibility. What has taken place over the years that has impacted the brokerage communities' credibility? In 1987 the stock market crashed, and inside trading scandals appeared all too frequently on the front page of the newspaper or on the evening news. There were also nearly 295,000 licensed representatives of all classifications in the securities industry as of December 31, 1983. As of June 30, 1994, this number has increased to 482,431. This increase, combined with negative media exposure, has led to the loss of credibility in the brokerage field. Too many prospects are the brunt of too many brokers making too many "cold calls" with only salesman status. Hence, the industry is perceived generically.

Consider this article from the financial newspaper, *Barron's*: "I have two brothers, one is a financial planner, the other was just sentenced to death for murder. My mother is a counterfeiter, my two sisters are ladies of the evening and my father is a hit man. Recently, I met a girl who was just released from a reformatory, where she served time for robbing a bank and using her child as a hostage. I want to marry her. My problem is, if I marry this girl, should I tell her about my brother, the financial planner?"

The legal profession is another example of losing credibility. The following statistics represent the number of lawyers in each country per 100,000 people.

- 11 in Japan
- 82 in England
- 111 in Germany
- 281 in the U.S.

More attorneys are providing what is too often perceived by the public as an industry of similar services. According to the American Bar Association Research Department, there are an estimated 862,954 lawyers in 1994 compared to 326,842 in 1970. The greater the numbers, the more generic the service is perceived. This concept has the ability to lower an industry's professional status.

The affluent group referred to earlier does not conduct business with anyone less than a professional. They do business with their attorneys, CPAs, and consultants who have achieved professional status and a higher level of competence.

Going the Distance

Relationships are defined in three ways: salesman, professional, or personal. The single word that distinguishes the difference between obtaining professional status or just being considered a salesman is *accountability*. Professionals go the distance in times of difficulty. If you are audited, you expect your CPA to follow through to its conclusion. On the other hand, when a salesman disappears in time of difficulty, you are not surprised.

To best illustrate a salesman relationship, look at how you purchase a used car. The feeling that comes over you when you see a used car salesman approaching is often one of distrust and annoyance. The reason your experiences create a basic distrust of the used car salespeople is because their reputation has generally been one of self interest.

A heart surgeon friend of mine who exemplifies professional status has developed a cardiac rehab facility providing post-cardiac care, counseling, dietary alternatives and many other services. Within the facility is a lap pool, which I use to swim seventy laps (one mile) for a good workout. When talking with recovering heart patients who use this facility, the first thing I notice is that all of them have been left with a scar from their surgery. They often ask me why I'm there, since I don't appear sick and don't bear the unmistakable chest scar. This enables me to explain that I'm there for preventative reasons, hoping to avoid coronary heart disease. I find them to be a particularly kind and sensitive group of people who now view their lives from a different perspective. They have slowed down in life, and at the very least, altered their focus. In conversation, I have asked them what they think of our mutual friend, the heart surgeon. Without exception, they have said that they hold him in the highest regard. They believe they would not be alive today without him. They perceive their heart surgeon as a professional and, in many cases, a personal friend. Conversely, I thought about how most of us perceive the used car salesperson. What an incredible dichotomy between the two occupations. If only all professions could develop the type of respect the heart surgeon has earned through his dedication, persistence, discipline, passion, and education, our careers would be so much easier.

Developing a personal connection with a client has one slim advantage over a professional association. However, it is difficult to develop a personal relationship with each client. Research advises you not to make this your primary focus. Do not attempt to develop a personal relationship with everyone with whom you do business. When that happens, make sure you are willing to pay the price of being a true friend, not just looking for business. Ultimately, you run the risk of losing your friendship, credibility, future business, and referrals. The affluent do not expect their CPA, attorney or advisors to be their best friend.

Who's in the Pool?

We should also ask ourselves why these men came to be in need of this cardiac rehabilitation center. If we stop and think of the reasons for these results, they probably stem back to a life out of balance in one or more aspects. Many of these men are considered typical type A personalities, excessive behavior oriented types who sacrificed their physical health and quality family time to achieve things they thought were important. Yet the consequences of these actions has, at the very least, altered their lifestyles, and, at worst, shortened their lives. Many people tell me that they don't have time to work out. To which I always respond: "If you don't have time to work out now, you'll have to take time to be sick later." I've never heard anyone on their death bed say they wish they'd spent more time working. Work, and a certain amount of stress associated with that work, is relatively healthy, productive, and stimulating. It creates the necessary challenges that push us to achieve the tasks put before us and to lead productive lives.

Webster defines *discipline*: "To gain or develop control through a system of rules or orderly conduct." The word *accountability* is defined as: "Having to be answerable to, or be responsible for, one's actions." These two words may be the basis for an orderly, successful transition through life.

We are all accountable for our behavior and the effect it has on our lives, as well as those immediately influenced by our actions. Lack of accountability is exhibited every day in courtrooms across America. The government continually expresses their inability to be accountable to its constituents through excessive spending and often exempting themselves from the same laws they impose upon us. Lack of discipline and accountability are the very essence of life's negative consequences. Not developing the right attitude toward these two areas of your life can result in ill health, failed businesses, failed relationships, crime, and disorder to name a few. Disciplining ourselves to eat properly, exercise, apply appropriate business ethics in our dealings with others (both personally and professionally), and budget our time and resources, all contribute to a properly balanced lifestyle.

Summary

You first have to be able to truly visualize what you want before you can achieve it. Recognize everyone is in sales and know the difference between selling and marketing. Position yourself to develop the skills to gain credibility through becoming an accountable and disciplined professional.

Chapter Two

Positioning Yourself to Succeed

"If you don't enjoy the climb, giving what it takes to get to the top isn't worth it."
— Malcolm S. Forbes, Sr.

I f we fail to make necessary changes, the next generation of adults may be the first not to achieve a lifestyle equal to or greater than that of their parents. To maintain or increase your standard of living, it is important to achieve *professional status.* It is imperative that you learn to *compete with your peers,* who may have already achieved professional status.

Is it possible to elevate your salesman status to professional status? Research tells us yes. It doesn't always happen; however, when it does, it can often take several years. Additionally, it takes five to twelve impressions to convert a prospect to a client. How you meet your prospect will largely determine your success and the amount of enjoyment you derive from the experience. Your success will always be in direct proportion to your ability to provide services or products and the ease with which you can, or cannot, be replaced. A specialist with extensive experience and education cannot be replaced as easily as someone with lesser skills or education.

Similar Products and Services

Organizations, individuals, and companies perceived by the public to provide similar products and services have a common problem setting themselves apart from their competition. Marketing your product or service to the affluent can be an obvious goal. When asked why he robbed banks Willie Sutton replied, "That's where the money is." If you earn $25,000 per year your market most likely falls into that same economic range. If you earn a six-figure income, you will generally deal with individuals or a market with proportionate needs. Your income usually mirrors the clientele to whom you are providing a product or service. While the average salesperson earns less than $40,000 per year, exceptional salespeople earn between $100,000 and $1,000,000 per year. Twenty-three years ago, my first sale in the brokerage industry was a $25 mutual fund to a young couple living in a trailer park, which is consistent with the above reference.

Any business has incredible highs and lows—that's the nature of the business world. Emotional ups and downs, whether they be in business, personal life, or the stock market, are all part of everyday life. Life is too short to convince a prospect that you are a good person in a world where there are far too few credible and accountable people. Your company is a good company in a world filled with equally struggling companies that are run by less than scrupulous, incompetent management. Your product is a good product and different in an environment plagued with inferior but similar products. Why then, should prospects change from what they have to what you are presenting? If they do, your problem then becomes overcoming the competition who are attempting to conserve their business. A difficult task, at the very least; and while sales is the highest paid profession in the world, it carries with it an equal degree of difficulty. If it were that easy, everyone would be successful. So how do we develop those specific skills necessary to break away from the crowd? An effective way of dealing with this circumstance is to learn how to compete with your peers.

Supermarket Mentality

To better understand how to compete with your peer group, we'll explore Procter and Gamble's research into public behavior and habits when buying tangible consumer products. In any grocery store, there is an aisle that has laundry detergents stacked among many other products. It's pretty difficult to miss this section, and the selection can be overwhelming. Try this test: Without help, name as many laundry detergents as you can. Studies suggest the average human mind cannot retain more than three to five items at one time and only those items in a high interest category. The average consumer can rarely name more than two or three product items or brand names, e.g., laundry detergent, toothpaste, and deodorant etc. On the other hand, the exception may be your spouse's ability to remember a thirteen digit credit card number, a definite high interest category. Like the shelves in a grocery store, you also have a shelf in your mind for each of these categories. Similarly, ask yourself how many of your prospects have a shelf in their mind for your services or products? In each case, they'll have a shelf containing three to five people or products. Procter and Gamble determined this concept decades ago. When it comes to selling a new toothpaste, they don't spend millions of dollars on prime time television advertising "great taste," "right price," or "it's new."

- To remain successful in continually marketing toothpaste requires offering _____ , the "Smoker's Toothpaste." As consumers, we don't have a shelf called "smokers toothpaste"; therefore, we create a new shelf called *Topol*.

- The soap for all your "2000 body parts," _____, we create a new shelf called *Lever 2000.*
- Most of us remember the advertisement "_____ tastes good like a _____should." Even though that commercial hasn't aired in more than twenty years, we still remember the slogan: "*Winston* tastes good like a *cigarette* should."
- Camel cigarette uses the character ____ Camel to set their product apart, using an image to whom people could relate, especially young people, who create a mental shelf for "*Joe Camel.*"
- The tartar control toothpaste _____ isn't just another toothpaste, it has peroxide and baking soda; therefore, we create a new shelf called "*Mentadent.*"

It is also easier to create a new shelf than knock someone off an existing shelf. Especially, if they have achieved professional or product status in an area where you may only be thought of as a generic salesman with a non-specialty product.

Apart from the Crowd

Another way to compete in today's world is through specialization. Successful people, almost without exception, specialize. This process creates power and increases your earning ability, thereby reducing the ease in which you can be replaced. For example there are two books on bar coding (scanning) which illustrate how specialization enables you to charge more for your product or service.

- *Market for Automatic Identification of Equipment* $2,700
- *World Bar Code Equipment Markets* $1,895

Many times you can specialize with similar procedures, products or services, providing what you are offering is limited or something that hasn't been heard or seen hundreds of times. Develop your skills in a market and provide a specialty product or service that fits your prospect's needs.

Psychologists tell us there are two important things in life. The first is to be loved and the second is to be understood.

> *"Attention is to people what*
> *fertilizer is to flowers."*
> — Malcolm S. Forbes, Sr.

We all have inherent problems in our businesses and lives. If someone comes along and specializes—takes the time to understand these problems and the inner workings of our business—it sets them apart from everyone else whose only goal is to make a sale. Creating a new shelf, almost without exception, is how successful people specialize.

An example of this is the introduction of an IPO (Initial Public Offering) of stock. Usually, the number of shares are limited. Consequently, restricting the number of people who may want to buy at the initial offering price. Therein lies a specialty—the ability to deliver a product or service. The worst time to buy an Initial Public Offering may be when you read about how great it is. On November 9, 1993, Boston Chicken went public and posted a 143 percent gain. If you had waited until November 10th, when every business page in America announced the opening day results, your value would have declined 7 percent from November 10 through March 16, 1994. Specialization in this context is the ability to deliver shares of a new stock offering the first trading day available.

Fear of Success

It is important, as professionals, that you know everything there is to know about the products and services you provide, including their politics, components, and competition. However, you must also know that a great deal of your success will be determined by the enthusiasm behind this knowledge. One trap I have seen many people fall into is the "fear of failure syndrome." They always have several special prospects who have large sales potential but are reluctant to call them for fear of losing them. The last time I checked, 100 percent of nothing is still nothing.

When I started in the securities business, because of my inexperience, a sales manager accompanied me on my first two calls and he lost both sales. I thought at the time, "I can do that." Thereafter, I depended on my own ability to learn. Ultimately, you will know more about a given product or market than you don't know. You will be able to consistently answer more objections, address more questions, and dramatically increase the probability of a productive conclusion. Initially, you will learn the most by buying your own product. It is very easy to become caught in the trap of being "afraid to succeed." Success, among many other things, carries with it a large degree of responsibility and commitment.

In fact, there is an advantage to starting at the bottom—one has no place to go but up! After a semester of college and having returned from Vietnam as a wounded infantry soldier, I borrowed $500 and bought a suit and a car. One day while driving down the street, my car started to lurch. The gas line had disconnected and the tank was careening down the street behind me. The floor of the trunk had rusted, disintegrated to the point where the gas tank had nothing to which to attach itself. I remember I opened the trunk in zero degree weather and looked down to the pavement. I extended steel bars from each side of the trunk that still contained some structure and tied steel wire around the gasoline tank to the two rods. Thereby I plugged the gas tank back in. The incident had punctured the tank, which prevented the purchase of no more than five dollars worth of gas. Times like these build character. Your attitude, commitment, and passion are the basic attributes that will move you toward your goals and dreams.

"Little Things Make Perfection..."

The amount of enthusiasm we garner in our everyday activities has a large impact on what we do and the success we achieve. Trial attorney F. Lee Bailey always said, "The case is never won in the courtroom, it is won in preparation." Knowing your product and practicing your presentation creates two major benefits. You will improve, and appear more professional and knowledgeable.

Consider this story. The artist Michaelangelo was working on his statue of David one afternoon when a friend stopped by. It appeared the sculpture had been completed, and Michaelangelo was finishing what many consider to be one of the most magnificent works of art ever created. Several months later, Michaelangelo's friend returned to find him still working on the same sculpture and said, "I thought you were finished?" Michaelangelo responded by saying, "Little things make perfection, but perfection is not a little thing."

Clock's Running

How do you start moving toward the lifestyle and markets in which you want to live and work, while increasing your earnings? You can begin to effectively accomplish this by allocating your time within different levels of potential income.

No matter what market you are in, it is included in one of the following groups. Before you will ever be successful in penetrating the higher income areas, you must understand what it takes to be successful at those levels. The $50,000 per year and below level is the fastest growing segment in America. It is a misconception that you start any business at entry level and automatically climb the ladder of success. In fact, there are several factors actually working against you in the opposite direction. However, if you understand why you do business at your present level, you will have the answers to propel you into the higher incomes.

$350,000 and Up	6 Months +	10%
$150,000 - $350,000	3-6 Months	15%
$50,000 - $150,000	90 Days	25%
$50,000 and Less	30 Days	50%

Some of the reasons you work at the lower levels may be:

- You already know the number of individuals at this level are greater and are easier to each.
- It is often your comfort zone because you don't like selling up; a less sophisticated market increases your comfort zone, particularly if you're more sophisticated than your marketplace.
- Salespeople are generally reluctant to call more successful clients without having the benefit of making all the mistakes on the less successful clients first.

- The lower level has fewer loyalties; they are not as structured as to with whom they do business as at the higher levels.

Your Comfort Zone

It may be obvious why you do business with the larger, less affluent segment of the market. There is one key point that enables you to elevate your level of business: can you reach your intended markets by expanding your comfort zone? The reason you fail to break into the higher markets is because you are out of your comfort zone. You can identify and reach the most comfortable bottom segment. Learn to grow by doing things you are most uncomfortable doing. As you expand your experience and confidence you increase your comfort zone.

The typical transaction size at this level generates a smaller sale. Therefore, you must complete many transactions to stay ahead. Although, there may come a time in your career where you continue to do as much business as you can, but you only have so much time in a day. You can only make so many presentations or provide so many products.

What happens to your income? It is going to decrease or plateau. In either case, one of two scenarios will develop. First, you are working sixteen hours a day and not willing to pay the price to continue, forcing you out of business. Consequently, the highest negative attrition rate is at this level. Secondly, you are working sixteen hours a day, you like the business, and you are going to continue doing what you are doing regardless of the sacrifices. You may think you will automatically climb the ladder of success, but this is not necessarily going to happen unless you understand certain forces that are at work.

The Habits of Success

Growth comes from getting out of your comfort zone and learning through experience by dealing with these higher level people. Also remember, the higher levels in the ladder do business with professionals. They exhibit more loyalty to the people with whom they regularly do business. Generally, if you get referrals from a professional, you are automatically perceived as a professional.

Most people getting into a business invariably start at the bottom, where everyone else is also struggling. When you begin to understand why you do business at a particular level, you will start to structure your life and your career accordingly.

Individuals and small companies generally operate monthly; although, it may seem to you that you operate on a longer cycle. Individuals earning less than $50,000 pay their mortgage, car payment, and most other bills on a monthly basis. Proportionately, people earning between $50,000 and $150,000 are more likely to think in terms of quarterly. Individuals at the $350,000 income level or higher generally operate in twelve-month intervals. Also, the largest commissions do not generally come in monthly. Most salespeople who immediately try to do business with the higher income levels run into difficulties. They realize they are not moving as fast as they want and become discouraged. Their rent or mortgage and car payments are due, and they fall back into their comfort zone. The secret is partially focusing on a longer term horizon and recognizing that there is a degree of pain involved in order to get out of your comfort zone.

Schedule a percentage of time every day to spend at each of these levels. Initially, a major portion of your time needs to be spent marketing at the bottom on a monthly basis to pay the bills. However, spend an increasing percentage of your time at the next level, where sales or a new market may take up to three months. If you have a restaurant, develop a catering business on the side, etc.

The next strata of sales, due to their sophistication, requires six months. The highest level may take a year or longer to conclude a transaction or develop a new market. Remember, big problems require specialization and generate big incomes. This same principle works not only for prospects, but also for referrals. The higher the levels of sophistication, for instance a CPA or attorney, the longer it may take for them to begin referring clients to you.

The Uphill Climb

Succeeding in business can have everything to do with whom you know, rather than what you know. Working smart in one or more of the following strategies will help you attain your goals.

- The first horse to ride is your company. Where is your company going? Or more impolitely, is it going anywhere at all? No matter how brilliant you are, it never pays to cast your lot with a loser. You can't do it yourself. If your company is going nowhere, get yourself a new one.

- The second horse to ride is your boss. Ask yourself the same questions about your boss as you asked yourself about your company. Is he or she going anywhere? If not, who is? Always try to work for the smartest, brightest, most competent person you can find. If you look at biographies of successful people, it's amazing to find how many crawled up the ladder of success right behind someone else. If your boss is going places, chances are good that you are too.

- The third horse to ride is a friend. Most of the big breaks that happen in a person's career happen because a business friend recommended that person. The way to ride the friendship horse is to keep in touch regularly with all your business friends.

- The fourth horse to ride is an idea. Everyone knows that an idea can take you to the top faster than anything else. But people sometimes expect too much of an idea. They want one that is not only great, but one that everyone else thinks is great too. There are no such ideas. If you wait until an idea is ready to be accepted, it's too late. You can't be first with a new idea or concept unless you are willing to stick your neck out. And take a lot of abuse. And bide your time until your time comes. Never be afraid of conflict.

- The fifth horse to ride is faith. Faith in others and their ideas. The importance of getting outside of yourself, of finding your fortune on the outside, is illustrated by the story of a man who was a failure most of his life. His name was Ray Kroc, and he was a lot older than most people and a failure to boot when he met two brothers who changed his life. For the brothers had an idea, but no faith. So they sold their idea as well as their name to Ray Kroc for relatively few dollars. Ray Kroc became one of the richest people in America. The brothers? They were the McDonald brothers, it was the vision, courage, and persistence of the outsider who made the McDonald's chain a success. Not two guys named McDonald.

- The sixth horse to ride is yourself. It is possible to succeed in business or in life all by yourself. But it's not easy. Like life itself, business is a social activity. As much cooperation as competition. The selling for example, you don't make a sale all by yourself. Somebody also has to buy what you're selling. So remember, the most success-ful jockeys are not necessarily the lightest, the smartest, or the strongest. The best jockeys don't win the race. The jockey that wins the race is usually the one with the best horse. So pick yourself a horse to ride and then ride it for all it's worth.

Summary

You cannot be all things to all people. Achieving professional status and specializing in specific markets and products enables you to maintain your focus and compete with your peers. By specializing and creating a shelf in your client's mind, it's much easier to provide additional services because your client has already perceived you as a professional. Meet your prospects in the most advantageous manner that increases your ability to succeed and minimizes frustration. It's important to understand where you are, and why you may feel comfortable. When you experience difficulties, resist the temptation to fall back into old habits. Organize your time effectively and work a percentage of your time in each market segment. Tackle all of this one step at a time. You will then be able you to get closer each day to attaining your life's goals.

Chapter Three

The People Mover

"Nothing can stop the man with the right mental attitude from achieving his goal, nothing on Earth can help the man with the wrong mental attitude."
—W. W. Siege

Several factors affecting your life and career are the management of people and problems. People who handle these areas maintain a more balanced life and career. The purpose of this chapter is to discuss how to deal with these issues by setting and accomplishing goals.

It is important to have a written plan. You need a longer, detailed plan spanning possibly three years or more, as well as an immediate plan covering the next twelve months. You'll also need to know how to accomplish these goals. Research indicates most people are not very good at planning. Most people spend less time planning their financial future than their annual vacation. The difficulty arises because most people don't know how to start planning. They don't know what questions to ask, much less know the answers. To achieve your objective, you must remain focused on your goal and increase your competence and effectiveness.

Four-Week Medical School

Establishing goals is an educational process which, hopefully, becomes a way of life. This may seem awkward at first. A professor in medical school, during his introduction to a new group of students, tells them he can teach them how to perform a successful medical procedure in four weeks. However, it may take him four years to teach them what to do if something goes wrong. This chapter is a little like the four-week course. It will point you in the right direction, but it's up to you to alter your habits and develop these skills as part of your life.

It is important to have short-term and long-term goals, and, most importantly, to write them down. If you only establish long-term goals (ones that may be out of reach in the normal course of life's ups and downs) you're missing the necessary reinforcement of short-term success. This may cause you to develop an "I can't seem to do it attitude" invariably defeating yourself in maintaining the enthusiasm and confidence to obtain any goal.

Short-term goals, those to be achieved within one year, need an immediate plan and require constant re-evaluation. These can help you grow by getting you out of your comfort zone. Long-range planning, at best, is difficult. Looking three to five years into the future poses a large degree of uncertainty, particularly in the changing world of business. It has been said that in business, as in life, if you are not progressing, you are regressing. It is comparable to rowing a boat upstream, you are either making progress or drifting backwards. There is no such thing as standing still.

Opportunity Knocks, Don't Forget to Answer the Door

It has been my experience that, as human beings, we don't understand the power of our subconscious. If we are subconsciously committed to a goal, we may not understand how we can achieve it. Because the objective is so far into the future, we can't get our arms around it at pivotal points in our lives. People usually create their own luck, which may simply mean to recognize an opportunity. I believe we bend the right way, at the right time, for the right reason, when we have a plan.

Conversely, short-term goals are necessary and the easiest to achieve because it is important to create a consistent pattern of success. It's a little like standing on top of an 11,325 foot mountain in Colorado, looking over the tips of your skis and wondering how in the world you are ever going to get to the bottom. I've found the only way to do this is by concentrating on just the fifteen feet in front of you, and then each fifteen feet after that. Before you know it, you've reached the bottom of the hill. That's when you realize you've just skied four miles, fifteen feet at a time!

Some things must be achieved one step at a time. Good or bad behavior can become a habit. It takes twenty-one days to change, or to reinforce, a behavior one small step at a time. Establishing short-term daily goals is important if you want to make a certain amount of income. For example, it is necessary to divide your goals into what needs to be accomplished per month, per week, and per day. Then learn the immediate task, or what needs to be achieved immediately. This is much easier than to lose focus of your twelve-month or three-to-five year goals when things don't always go the way you want. Doing this on a daily basis may simply mean making a certain number of calls per day or seeing two people per day or selling X number of items per day. Days turn into weeks, weeks into months, months into years, and years into lifetime accomplishments. Doing things one step at a time requires remaining focused and being persistent. You will achieve your goals. I'm not just talking about goals in the context of financial success. Your goals should also include personal goals concerning your health, family, friends, spirituality, and professional life.

WAL★MART's Way

The late Sam Walton, who started with nothing and proceeded to build WAL★MART and one of America's greatest fortunes, wrote these ten principles to follow in business:

- Rule 1: Commit to your business. Believe in it more than anybody else. I think I overcame every single one of my personal shortcomings by sheer passion I brought to my work.

- Rule 2: Share your profits with all your associates, and treat them as partners, and together you will perform beyond your wildest expectations.

- Rule 3: Motivate your partners. Money and ownership alone are not enough. Constantly think of new and more interesting ways to motivate and challenge your partners. Set high goals, encourage competition, and then keep score. Make bets with outrageous payoffs. If things get stale, cross pollinate; have managers switch jobs with one another to stay challenged. Keep everybody guessing as to what your next trick is going to be. Don't become too predictable.

- Rule 4: Communicate everything you possibly can to your partners. The more they now, the more they will understand. The more they understand, the more they'll care. Once they care, there's no stopping them from succeeding. If you don't trust your associates to know what's going on, they'll know you don't really consider them partners. Information is power, and the gain you get from empowering your associates more than offsets the risk of informing your competition.

- Rule 5: Appreciate everything your associates do for the business. A paycheck and a stock option will only buy one kind of loyalty. All of us like to be told how much we are appreciated. We like to hear it often, and especially when we have done something of which we're really proud. Nothing else can quite substitute for a few well-chosen, well-timed, sincere words.

- Rule 6: Celebrate your successes. Find some humor in your failures. Loosen up, and everybody around you will loosen up. Have fun. Always show enthusiasm. When all else fails, put on a costume and sing a silly song. Then make everybody else sing with you. Think up your own stunt. All of this is important (and more fun) than you think, and it really fools the competition into thinking, why should we take these guys seriously?

- Rule 7: Listen to everyone in your company and figure out ways to get them talking. The folks on the front, the ones who actually talk to the customer, are the only ones who really know what's going on out there. Find out what they know. To push responsibility down into your organization, and to force good ideas to bubble up within it, you must listen to what your associates are trying to tell you.

- Rule 8: Exceed your customer's expectations. If you do, they'll come back many times over. You should give them what they want and a little more. Let them know you appreciate them. Make good on all your mistakes; don't make excuses, apologize. Stand behind everything you do. The two most important words I ever wrote on the first WAL★MART sign: Satisfaction Guaranteed. They're still up there, and they make all the difference in the world.

- Rule 9: Control your expenses better than your competition. This is where you can always find the competitive advantage. For twenty-five years running, our company had the lowest ratio of expenses to sales. You can make a lot of mistakes and still recover if you can run an efficient operation. You can also be brilliant and still go out of business if you're too inefficient.

- Rule 10: Swim upstream. Go the other way. Ignore the way everybody else may be doing something. There's a good chance you can find your niche by going in exactly the opposite direction. In all my years, the one piece of advice I heard more often than any other was, a town of less than 50,000 population cannot support a discount store for very long.

The Reward of Responsibility

Internal items which you can control consist of your behavior toward problems, utilizing your strengths and recognizing your weaknesses. External items you cannot control involve the economy, legislation, world events, and your competition. Good planning minimizes that which we cannot control. I'm sure we can all cite many situations, maybe from our own lives, that are managed from crisis to crisis. The government has a tendency to operate this way. Dr. Norman Vincent Peale said: "It is the reaction to life's crisis, rather than the crisis itself, that is most important."

Planning teaches you to prioritize areas of your life. You need to better learn how to delegate items that can be done effectively by others and concentrate on items you feel you do best. President Carter tried to do to much himself, while President Reagan delegated too much. Both had problems caused by their different styles of government. A balance of these qualities is best. Concentrate on those qualities which make you different from everyone else. Formulation is not concerned with future decision, but rather the impact current decisions have on the future. Preparation is also not intended to reduce risk. Indeed, risk is a necessary part of success; it enables you to take the right risk at the right time for the right reason.

The major risk factors are: **health, family, and failure**. Most professions can take a heavy emotional toll on you because of anxiety which can develop into ill health. Most people worry about everything. However, about 90 percent of everything we are distressed about never comes to pass.

There are also risks associated with your family. The high divorce rate in this country confirms this fact. The planning process allows a balance between a successful career and a successful family.

The ultimate risk is failure. Good planning and communication will help you stabilize all of these areas. Preparation allows you to formalize your concept of the future.

Flight Plan

Formulation also enables you to envision goals which cannot be achieved until you can first perceive them in your mind and put them on paper. Not committing your goals to writing is like flying an airplane without a flight plan. It is important to write these goals down in confidence and be honest with yourself, so you are not writing something you want others to think you are. It is important that your plan identifies your strengths and weaknesses so you can honestly deal with the process, no matter how painful it may be. You are really three types of people:

- The person you really are
- The person you want to be
- The person you want others to think you are

Balancing responsibility will determine your happiness and success, and will be in direct correlation to the amount of time you spend formulating and establishing your goals. Both success and failure can be barriers to goal achievement. Can you be too successful or too unsuccessful to plan? The problem with successful people is they may feel they no longer need goals, which can cause them to fail. Unsuccessful people often feel they don't have time to establish goals.

It's important that your goals are realistic. They should be written and reviewed frequently. Make them suit your self-image and your purpose in life. Use goals to reward yourself, whether in a big or small way. Rewards can be constructive, positive and healthy, or destructive. For example, instead of rewarding yourself with addictive behavior, change your behavior toward a positive reinforcement.

Be careful with what you put in your goal book. It just may come true! When I started in business with absolutely nothing, I made a goal to purchase a Rolls Royce. Several years later, I purchased a new Silver Shadow and paid cash. Only after purchasing the Rolls did I realize it was the wrong place and time in my life. Let possessions into your life with reservation and only after careful consideration.

20/20 Vision

Problems are part of every day life and business. If you don't have any obstacles, you're probably not involved in much. Goals will help you overcome these areas.

Where would General Schwartzkopf be without Saddam Hussein? Where would Lee Iacocca be without Chrysler? Fortunately, problems will only end when we do. Everyone has problems concerning people, money, product, and growth—the list can be endless. Just as the answers are always in the question, great opportunities always lie in the problems. Yet, if all of this is true, why do we react so poorly when difficulties arise? Part of the reason may be an immature response to obstacles and the failure to think about them. Instead of anticipating complications, welcome them as growth opportunities.

When difficult decisions arise, I often divide a piece of paper in half and list all the positives on one side and all the negatives on the other. Invariably, I find this helps me make a decision. It also helps me keep in perspective that there are, generally, more positives than negatives in which to be thankful.

Developing an attitude toward a problem means taking action. The difference between success and failure is how you deal with difficulties when they present themselves. Good businesses have challenging problems; bad businesses have crippling ones. It is the art of management that makes them so interesting, often attracting the best and brightest people. Learn to be interested and fascinated, not paralyzed, by them and realize every negative holds a solution or opportunity. Create an environment that attracts and retains bright, articulate, and intelligent problem-solvers. The bigger your problems, and the better you are at solutions, the more they will provide you with greater success. It has been said that problems house the profits of the future. The ability to solve bigger issues enables you to specialize and achieve the higher income levels, making you more difficult to replace.

You need to develop a strategy for dealing with problems. Determine the facts, sort out the real issues, and think about possible solutions. Doctors, accountants, and lawyers have a systematic and effective way of doing this.

- Perform tests
- Analyze information
- Offer solutions
- Extend diagnoses
- Create conclusions

It is important you alter your sense of time and urgency in order to deal with difficulties effectively. Try to remain calm, which can be initially difficult. Calmness and courage are learned responses. Anything short of bodily damage won't hurt you.

The greatest problem-solving skill, calmness, can be developed by addressing the following points.

- Who, where, why and what are the real problems?
- What are the consequences of inaction?
- Do I need to respond or will the problem go away?
- Who else, if anyone, needs to be involved?
- Formulate a response
- Decide if you need a short- or long-term solution
- Outline steps
- Try not to respond in anger

When implementing these steps, make sure the problem gets solved, or assigned to a capable person for follow-up. But remember, you are ultimately accountable, and the difference between a salesman and a professional is accountability.

Back to Work By 3 PM

Did you ever notice that everyone goes back to work by 3 p.m. after a funeral? Norman Vincent Peale once met a man who said he was tormented by problems. Peale replied that he, himself, just came from a place where there were 60,000 people without any problems. The man responded with excitement. "I'd like to be there!" Peale replied: "I don't think you would. It's called Wood-lawn Cemetery."

The enemy of success is pessimism. The philosopher Hegel wrote: "Of one thing I am certain, nothing is accomplished without passion. Passion creates the iron will and indomitable spirit needed to grow and develop your business, as well as the people in it who solve your problems. Passion makes you authentic, and authenticity breeds integrity. Integrity, in return, attracts people."

One of Winston Churchill's greatest commencement speeches may also be the shortest on record. When he stood up in front of the graduating class, they were understandably filled with anticipation and anxious to hear the wisdom imparted to them by Churchill at the beginning of their adult journey. After he stood, Churchill paused for a moment, then stated, "Never give up, never give up, never give up!" Then he sat down, to the amazement of everyone in the audience. He, indeed, was truly a wise man. When things get difficult, maybe some of the following true stories will help you to "never give up."

- Possibly the greatest NBA basketball star ever, Chicago Bull's Michael Jordan, was cut from the basketball team his sophomore year in high school.

- After reviewing Disney's first drawings for consideration, an editor told Walt Disney he had no talent.

- An employer said that W.F. Woolworth did not have sufficient common sense in dealing with the public and prevented Woolworth from waiting on customers.

- Babe Ruth will be remembered for his 714 home runs and not for the 1,330 time he struck out. Ty Cobb will be remembered for stealing an incredible ninety-six bases in one season—not for the thirty-eight times he was thrown out in the attempt.

- Dan Jansen lost in six Olympic speed-skating races before he won the seventh race of his Olympic career, earning a gold medal in the 1,000 meter event.

- Joe Montana, conceivably the greatest quarterback in football history was benched his junior year in high school. He started his college career as a seventh string backup at Notre Dame.

When somebody says you can't do something, consider these preposterous statements.

- "Who the hell wants to hear actors talk?"
—Harry M. Warner, Warner Brothers Pictures, in 1927.
- "Sensible and responsible women do not want to vote."
—Grover Cleveland, U.S. president, in 1905.

Summary

Set your goals and strive to achieve them in your personal and professional life. Make your own luck by establishing successful habits. Be realistic in your expectations, be honest with yourself and, most importantly, write your goals down on paper.

Develop the methods outlined to deal with your problems and welcome them as opportunities. Lighten up on yourself, take one step at a time toward your objectives, and never give up.

Chapter Four

Managing Your Finances

*"The man who follows the crowd will
never be followed by a crowd."*
—Donnell

The late Bernard Baruch, a famous economist, was asked in
an interview what he thought would happen to the stock
market. He responded: "I think the market will go up and down."
Understanding the market and, in the process, developing a discipline to accumulate and maintain wealth net of inflation and
taxes is the purpose of this chapter. There are always those who
are confident that we are nowhere near the top of the market.
While others expect the market to crash by the end of the year. I
am most comfortable when there's a consensus, either positive or
negative, in the stock market because, invariably, the market will
generally go in the opposite direction. The market is difficult to
determine when there is fairly equal division among the bulls
(rising trend) and bears (declining trend), when it can go either
way. In my experience, the stock market will generally do whatever it has to do to prove the vast majority of investors wrong.

Today there are millions of Americans pouring money into
the stock market at an unprecedented rate via mutual funds.
Mutual funds are increasingly the basis of many people's savings. This trend is a definite cultural shift. One in every four
American home owners invests in mutual funds.

The first publicly traded mutual fund was established in
1924. The number of mutual funds available to the public grew

to 458 by 1980, and currently exceeds 5,375. According to the Investment Company Institute, total mutual fund assets under management grew from $58.4 billion in 1980 to $2.1 trillion in 1994. More mutual funds are available today than all of the stocks in the New York Stock Exchange.

Baby Boomers Grow Up

This trend has been largely created by a whole new generation of baby boomers who have grown out of their spending years, i.e., purchasing homes, cars, etc., and into their saving years, funding retirement accounts, i.e., mutual funds, stocks, bonds, and annuities. While they have replaced their jogging shoes for walking shoes, they seek greater appreciation for their investments other than returns available through savings accounts.

When investing in the stock market, one's expectations should be in relative, not absolute, returns. What I mean is, in the early 1980s, when the market was experiencing double-digit inflation and double-digit fixed interest rates, it wasn't unreasonable to anticipate proportionately higher returns in the equities market. It is important you adjust these expectations to different times. This is particularly the case today where we are experiencing 3 to 4 percent inflation and 4 to 6 percent fixed interest returns. Consequently, one's expectations and returns in the equities market should be proportionate.

Today the average professional spends over 2,000 hours a year doing what he does best to make a living, and less than five hours a year planning his or her financial future. The fact we now live in an electronic, global society with virtually twenty-four-hour trading days, has made it easy to forget what the industry was like just a few years ago.

It is important not to lose sight of why and how people should invest. In 1986, trading on the New York Stock Exchange exceeded one trillion shares for the first time in its history. In perspective, one trillion seconds amounts to 32,000 years. This number was once again exceeded, in an even shorter time, on October 19, 1987, when the Dow dropped 508 points; and 615 million shares were traded in a single day. In light of current technology and investment alternatives, a long-term basic value investment philosophy has often been replaced by the more popular immediate-gain philosophy. History reminds us that capital preservation, reasonable growth and longer-term investment horizons have yielded consistent gains. Selecting unpopular investments with healthy balance sheets and moderate debt, those discounted relative to the market, support this theory. In good times, we all have a tendency to follow the path of least resistance and get away from these values. Going back to basic principles allow us to remember and apply sound investment traditions into tomorrow.

The stock market has been, and will remain, volatile and unpredictable, driven by either greed or fear in the short term. However, in the long term, the stock market has historically been a good hedge against inflation while gradually drifting upward.

This chapter will sort through the stock market and show how mutual funds can be used to achieve financial independence.

A Few Good Men

How do you find a good broker? In my experience, one of the best ways to determine whether a broker is working in your best interest is to inquire as to their ownership of the investment they are suggesting. Regardless of how large or small their participation may be, if they think it's good enough for you, they should want to own the same investment.

As a young mutual fund wholesaler for the Pioneer Fund in my early twenties, I was fortunate enough to spend time with Philip Carret, who founded the Pioneer Mutual Fund in 1928. He remains on the board today and, at the age of ninety-seven, still runs Carret & Co., his investment firm in New York. He has lived through thirty-one bull markets, thirty bear markets, twenty recessions, and the depression. Phil shared with me his philosophy on investing, which I have carried with me my entire career. He said,

- "Avoid consumer debt on depreciating assets, when possible."

For example financing clothing, home furnishings, appliances, electronic equipment, and vacations that decline in value as opposed to appreciate in value.

The Plastic Nightmare

Consumer credit card debt has reached epidemic proportions in this country and compromises the very financial future of many families. Credit is extended, in many cases, with little consideration of the consumer's ability to repay. Then, when difficulties arise, additional credit can often be obtained, further exacerbating the problem. Few people realize that if only the minimum payment is made on a credit card with a $10,000 balance at 20 percent, it will take thirty years to eliminate the debt, including $16,249 of interest. Thus, the total repayment obligation then equals $26,249. Interest on these credit cards can range as high as 20 percent, which is no longer deductible. If you realize that once you pay your credit balances and discontinue the use of these cards, you will have all of the discretionary income generally paid in principle and interest to use as cash. Granted, there may be times when the controlled convenience of a credit card is a necessity, as long as it doesn't get out of control.

There are effective ways to eliminate credit card debt. First destroy and cancel all of your credit cards. You don't necessarily have to carry the card in your pocket to use it. When you don't have them available, somehow you make do without them. Next itemize your credit cards in descending order, and give those with higher interest rates the top priority. Continue to pay the minimum balance on all of your cards. Each time you eliminate a card, add the minimum financial obligation of that card to the payment of the next card, and so on. This process accelerates the reduction of debt. One additional advantageous method of accelerating debt reduction is paying an additional amount of money. Each month, this will accelerate and eliminate your situation more quickly, with exceptional savings in interest costs. After adopting a sound philosophy concerning debt, a contrarian view of the market can assist you in achieving other financial goals.

Wall Street Week

Phil Carret's investment philosophy also included the following,

- "Stick to the basics (keep it simple) with high-quality companies with strong balance sheets where the management is substantially invested in their own company.
- The company should also have modest debt and substantial cash reserves.
- Invest a substantial percentage of your assets into good quality, diversified equities.
- Invest for the long term in companies you understand.
- Invest a small percentage of your assets (three to five percent) into gold and silver as a hedge against inflation.
- Avoid fades and following the crowd."

The following is an excerpt from *Wall Street Week* of an interview between Louis Rukeyser and Phil Carret which further discusses the market.

Rukeyser: Phil, what are you doing right?

Carret: We try to apply common sense to the problem of investing.

Rukeyser: Well, let's start with what we just looked at. How do you feel about this increased emphasis on yields which we are hearing about from all sides these days?

Carret: I am a great believer in the total return theory.

Rukeyser: Are you buying more bonds now than you used to?

Carret: No. I think an individual should have a certain backlog of bonds, but primarily, the money is made in stocks. One can't make money without owning something.

Rukeyser: You said you had succeeded by applying common sense, that's an uncommon prescription. How do you apply common sense to a market that has been as erratic as this one has been over the last five or twenty years?

Carret: Try to buy basic value stocks, stocks of companies with good assets, small or no liabilities other than current liability, good earnings records and rising dividends—preferably not too high.

Rukeyser: You have gained attention over the years, not only because you scoffed at short-term stock market predictions, I think more and more people are doing that, but because you have said you are always buying stocks. Now why do you do that?

Carret: We believe in being fully invested at all times, because this means that, in reference to the general market, one third of the time we may be wrong...

Rukeyser: You suggested, Phil, that it was always very easy, common sense you said, and you also have given us some of the guidelines you use in picking stocks, but you have also suggested other people don't have much common sense. You suggested that you don't buy the kinds of stocks that other people are buying. Why is that?

Carret: I don't think that it is a question so much of common sense—it is a crowd philosophy. It is very difficult to go counter to what the general crowd is thinking and doing, and perhaps, over the years, I have trained myself to be skeptical of the crowd mind.

Rukeyser: You said once that you would sell a stock if too many people recommended it. How does that work?

Carret: Well, if too many people are recommending it, probably the stock is high and is probably not a bargain. A bargain is when they are neglected.

Rukeyser: While the average person watching this program may think, By the time I hear about it, it will probably be too late. Is that true? Does the small investor have a chance?

Carret: I think the small investor has a very good chance if he will buy a good stock, sit with it and live a long time.

Rukeyser: You don't always just sit on it, do you? What are the signals to lead you to sell a stock?

Carret: I prefer somebody to take it away from me by a merger or a tender offer, or something like that.

Rukeyser: Are the stocks in your funds, say the Pioneer Fund which goes back half a century, in the course of a year is your turnover less than that of most mutual funds? Do you sell fewer stocks?

Carret: I think we do. Our turnover is between 15 and 20 percent.

Rukeyser: Now, again, translating what you do into the terms of an average small investor, you are saying "look for companies that have conservative balance sheets, that don't have too high an earnings price ratio, that are not institutional favorites." What are some of the other guidelines?

Carret: That they are well managed.

Rukeyser: How can an outsider judge that?

Carret: Well, there is just one very simple criteria which
              I apply and that is the extent to which the man-
              agement has its own money in the business. If
              the president of the company, as happened in
              one stock a few years ago in which he had an
              interest in 200 shares is getting a $20 stock and
              receiving $105,000 in salary, I would think he
              didn't have enough confidence in the company.
              Would you?

Rukeyser: Fair enough. And you feel that, once finding that
              kind of stock, you should sit on it forever, or
              until when?

Carret: Pretty nearly forever, yes.

(At this point, Dan Dorfman enters into the interview and
asks Mr. Carret "Based on your experience, if you could give
investors just one single piece of advice, what would that advice
be?")

Carret: Have patience. It takes time. The Chinese say
              "The tree does not grow to heaven and it takes a
              long time to grow a couple hundred feet"...

Rukeyser: In your judgment, why is the market behaving so
              nervously right now?

Carret: Well, I think it is largely due to Washington. By
              and large we get no good news from Washington

except when Congress adjourns and they adjourn far too infrequently.

Rukeyser: Looking into the future, do you feel optimistic about the American economy?

Carret: Yes, I have traveled all over the world pretty extensively and the American people are a great, productive people who still believe in themselves and their country, and have a great confidence in the future despite the constant nibbling at the edges of the economy, which government does. But so far businessmen have been able to circumvent them to a major degree.

The interesting thing about this interview is that it was taped September 9, 1977, which is evidence that history repeats itself.

Excuses, Excuses

Historically, there have always been reasons not to invest in the stock market. You only need to read the headlines or watch the nightly news. Political and economic events that affect the market are such that, arguably, you could come up with a reason not to invest at any given time. A look back at history through the covers of various *Newsweek* magazines further illustrates this point.

- May 4, 1970   Now It's The Indochina War
- April 17, 1972   The War That Won't go Away (Vietnam)
- September 17, 1973   Arab Oil Squeeze

- January 20, 1975   Out Of Work
- April 5, 1976   Nixon's Final Days
- February 7, 1977   The Gas Crisis
- May 29, 1978   Inflation
- March 31, 1980   The Credit Crunch
- February 23, 1981   Are We Running Out Of Water?
- May 10, 1982   The War Is On (The Falkland Islands)
- November 7, 1983   Americans At War (U.S. Paratroopers in Grenada)
- July 1, 1985   Ten Ways To Fight Terrorism
- November 2, 1987   After The Crash (The Stock Market Crash In October)
- January 30, 1989   Can You Afford To Get Sick? (The Battle Over Health Benefits)
- May 21, 1990   Bonfire Of The S & L's (How Much You Will Pay And Are The Banks Next)?
- January 7, 1991   Saddam Hussein; More Than Just A Madman
- July 26, 1993   Deluge; Lessons Of A Disaster (Referencing The Midwest Floods)
- April 11, 1994   How To Survive In A Scary Market

You have to first determine whether you are a pessimist or an optimist to live with the market. The pessimist always sees the negative news and sits on the side line; the optimist always sees the opportunity and invests which can create long term wealth.

In 1988 John Templeton (the founder of the Templeton funds), made several interesting observations and comments about long-term prosperity that still ring true today.

"I don't think there are any more problems today than any of the forty-eight years since I became an investment counselor in 1940. The world is now spending about one billion dollars every business day on scientific research. Half of all the scientists who ever lived are alive today. Doctors at the beginning of this century had only one-tenth the knowledge that medicine now has. The average life span is two times greater than two centuries ago. Two centuries ago, 85 percent of the world's people were needed to produce enough food. Now, in America, fewer than 4 percent are producing food. This scientific research results in greater production, better quality, lower costs, greater variety. In my lifetime, the world's standard of living has quadrupled, after accounting for inflation. That is the first time in any life history that the standard of living has quadrupled. Our studies indicate that the standard of living is going to quadruple again in the next forty years instead of the next seventy years. We are living in the most glorious period of world history, we are looking ahead toward an extraordinary period of long-term prosperity."

Given this backdrop, ask yourself three questions concerning your financial future.

- Are your investments generating an acceptable return, net of inflation and taxes?
- Are your investments going to enable you to achieve your financial goals?
- What is the largest financial obstacle you face in the future?

The following points are important in accumulating and conserving wealth:

- To win, the first thing you have to do is not lose.
- Preservation of capital is a key element in wealth accumulation.
- Not taking risks may be the biggest risk of all.

It is an unfortunate commentary that, at age 65, in the wealthiest country in the world, out of every 100 people according to the Social Security Administration:

- 34 are deceased
- 54 are financially broke
- 5 are still working
- 4 are financially independent
- 1 is wealthy

The reasons for these statistics are infinitely more complex, but basically amount to the following:

- They don't have a plan.
- They use the wrong investments.
- They allow their emotions to influence their financial decisions.
- They don't understand the effects of compound interest, taxes, and inflation.

In order to achieve financial independence, you need to understand and apply the following five rules of wealth accumulation:

- Develop a plan.
- Establish your goals.
- Use fundamentally sound investments.
- Understand compound interest, taxes, and inflation.
- Remove emotion from your financial decisions.

These principles can provide the foundation on which to build your financial future and create long-term prosperity.

When to Buy and Sell

The most difficult part of the equation of buying and selling may be knowing when to sell a stock, not falling in love with it, or getting otherwise emotionally involved. Buying mutual funds can, essentially, remove the sell side of this equation. After selecting a diversified group of funds which meet your criteria and objectives, the most important element then becomes holding on to them in good and bad economic times. You may want to sell a fund only if there has been a change in management, the funds, or your philosophy and goals. Warren Buffett, who is worth $8 billion, says that his favorite holding period for stocks is forever. He picks stocks carefully and hates to sell them.

There are two basic things you can do with money. You can **loan** your money to the bank in the form of certificates of deposit, treasury bills, and earn interest in the process. The bank subsequently loans out this money via mortgages, installment loans, personal loans, etc., at a higher rate of return. Secondly, you can **own** your money by investing in equities which represent a cross-section of assets in American or international companies, thereby generating potential appreciation and hedging the risk of inflation.

Compromising Positions

First, it is important to understand that inflation has, and will always be, an inherent part of democracy. We have lived with inflation for fifty of the past fifty-two years. Historically, it has not really mattered whether a democrat or republican has been in the White House. Democrats have a tendency to spend money on people (entitlement programs), while republicans have a tendency to spend money on defense. Both programs are inflationary. The only difference is that defense spending creates jobs and a stronger military presence in the world, while entitlement programs create a more welfare-oriented society.

Secondly, saving account yields have traditionally mirrored inflation (not considering taxes). If the account is subject to taxes, a loss of purchasing power is likely to occur. Adjusted for inflation, the worst 30-year period for stock returns since 1926 was better than the best 30-year period for T-Bonds. The following chart illustrates the real return, after inflation, on an annualized average monthly rate for a six-month certificate of deposit through August 1994. These rates of return, net of inflation (Source: Federal Reserve Board), yield, in some cases, a negative real return.

YEAR	6 MO. CD	INFLATION	RETURN
1970	7.65	5.5	2.15
1971	5.21	3.4	1.81
1972	5.02	3.4	1.62
1973	8.31	8.8	(0.49)
1974	9.98	12.2	(2.22)
1975	6.89	7.0	(0.11)
1976	5.62	4.8	0.82
1977	5.92	6.8	(0.88)
1978	8.61	9.0	(0.39)
1979	11.44	13.3	(1.86)
1980	12.99	12.4	0.59
1981	15.77	8.9	6.87
1982	12.57	3.9	8.67
1983	9.27	3.8	5.47
1984	10.68	4.0	6.68
1985	8.25	3.8	4.45
1986	6.50	1.1	5.40
1987	7.01	4.4	2.61
1988	7.85	4.4	3.45
1989	9.08	4.6	4.48
1990	8.24	6.1	2.14
1991	5.60	3.1	2.50
1992	3.50	3.2	0.30
1993	2.66	2.4	0.26
1994	4.42	3.3	1.12

The next chart indicates a CD net of taxes and inflation from 1970 through August 1994.

YEAR	6 MO. CD	TAX RATE	INFLATION	RETURN
1972	5.02	70.00	3.41	(1.90)
1973	8.31	70.00	8.80	(6.31)
1974	9.97	70.00	12.20	(9.21)
1975	6.89	70.00	7.01	(4.94)
1976	5.62	70.00	4.81	(3.12)
1977	5.92	70.00	6.77	(4.99)
1978	8.61	70.00	9.03	(6.45)
1979	11.44	70.00	13.31	(9.88)
1980	12.94	70.00	12.40	(8.52)
1981	15.79	70.00	8.94	(4.20)
1982	12.57	50.00	3.87	2.42
1983	9.28	50.00	3.80	0.84
1984	10.71	50.00	3.95	1.41
1985	8.24	50.00	3.77	0.35
1986	6.50	50.00	1.13	2.12
1987	7.01	38.50	4.41	(0.10)
1988	7.91	33.00	4.42	0.88
1989	9.08	33.00	4.65	1.43
1990	8.17	33.00	6.11	(0.64)
1991	5.91	31.00	3.06	1.02
1992	3.50	31.00	3.20	(0.79)
1993	2.66	39.60	2.40	(0.79)
1994	4.42	39.60	3.30	(0.63)

The accumulative rate of return during the past nearly twenty-three years has created a loss of purchasing power of -52 percent and an average total negative return of -2.28 percent per year. Showing CD returns in 1981 of nearly 16 percent which maintained purchasing power less than the return in 1994 of 4.42 percent. We are better off today, we just don't feel good about it. However, CDs are only one of many types of investments whose returns are affected negatively by taxes and inflation. CDs are guaranteed as to timely payment of both principal and interest and have fixed principal and return values if held to maturity.

However, it is important to establish a basis of these types of assets. A comfortable portion of your assets should be placed in the bank, despite the effects of taxes and inflation, for liquidity purposes, emergency funds, short-term education requirements, or any other financial contingency. It is equally important to have liquid assets (maybe six months of income) before considering alternate investments. There are worse things than 3 to 5 percent yields. There is no exact science in determining the percentage of your assets which should be considered for equities. However, a rule of thumb is to subtract your age from 100 as a percentage to keep in stocks or stock mutual funds. Before you apply this formula, determine your obligations in the next five years, including emergency funds, college obligations and any other expense to be kept in cash equivalents such as money market accounts, CDs, etc. After comfortably establishing the basis for your portfolio, employing compound interest is the most fundamental tool to achieve financial independence.

Double Your Money?

One of the basic rules of finance will help us understand how your money, or cost of living, will double. The Rule of 72 is a hypothetical compounding equation that does not represent the return of any particular investment. The returns of most investments fluctuate over time, no one can predict with certainty when an investment will double in value.

YOUR MONEY, OR COST OF LIVING, WILL DOUBLE

- At 4 percent it will take 18 years for one dollar to double
- At 4 percent inflation it will take 18 years for your cost of living to double

- At 6 percent it will take 12 years for one dollar to double
- At 9 percent it will take 8 years for one dollar to double

These figures are achieved by simply dividing the interest rate into 72, which equals the number of years it takes for one dollar to become two dollars. It has been said that Einstein could understand $E=MC^2$ but could not grasp compound interest, which he called the Eighth Wonder of the World.

A $10,000 investment for twenty years at 4.5 percent would earn $14,117 in interest, for a total of $24,117 (not considering taxes or inflation). If you doubled the 4.5 percent return to 9 percent, you might assume you would double the $14,117 of interest to $28,234 plus principal for a value of $38,234. The correct answer is $56,044 accumulated through the benefit of compound interest illustrated below.

RATE OF RETURN
$10,000 X 20 YEARS @ 4.5%:
$10,000 ORIGINAL PRINCIPAL
$14,117 INTEREST RATE 4.5%
$24,117 TOTAL

DOUBLE YOUR RATE OF RETURN
$10,000 X 20 YEARS @ 9%:
4.5% + 4.5% = 9%
$10,000 ORIGINAL PRINCIPAL
$28,234 ($14,117 + $14,117)
$38,234 TOTAL

CORRECT ANSWER $56,044

The following chart illustrates a variety of costs today and what they may be at an assumed 5 percent inflation rate (using an energy inflation factor of 8 percent and a medical inflation rate of 12 percent) in ten, twenty, and thirty years.

	TODAY	10 YEAR	20 YEARS	30 YEARS
AUTOMOBILE	$20,000	$32,577	$53,066	$86,439
CONDO	$100,000	$162,889	$265,329	$432,194
VACATION	$3,500	$5,701	$9,287	$15,127
GOLF GAME	$85	$138	$226	$1,512
DOCTOR VISIT	$35	$57	$93	$151
HEALTH CARE	$2,496	$7,752	$24,072	$74,784
PRESCRIPTION	$45	$140	$434	$1,348
PROPERTY TAX	$1,500	$2,443	$3,980	$6,483
GASOLINE	$1.10	$2.37	$5.13	$11.07
AIR FARE	$500	$1,079	$2,330	$5,031
ELECTRIC BILL	$125	$270	$583	$1,258
PHONE CALL	$1.25	$2.04	$3.32	$5.40

History painfully illustrates that we cannot afford to leave all our money in fixed income type accounts. It would also not be prudent to put all our money into equities or any single investment. I would encourage most people looking for long-term appreciation and a hedge against inflation to consider mutual funds. How do you estimate how long you want your money to work for you? Determine a tolerance for risk that will enable you to sleep comfortably at night. Also familiarize yourself with mutual fund fee structures, track records, consistency of performance, and management.

The College Crunch

Not long ago, the largest investment most families worried about was buying a house. However, today's educational costs continue to outpace the general inflation rate. A college or graduate school education is becoming one of the largest financial commitments families will make. Calculating future education expenses can be frightening. Since 1980, the cost of a college education has risen twice as fast as prices in general.

- Today, a freshman year at a state university might cost $9,000 to $12,000.
- Yet, for a child born today, his freshman year at a projected 6 percent annual inflation rate might cost between $26,500 to $35,400.
- Total four year cost could be between $106,000 and $141,600.

This is certainly a formidable goal. The following methods can help you achieve this.

- The yearly investment to achieve $106,000 would require $2,515 to have enough to cover your costs. This is assuming seventeen years to go before entering a four year school that currently costs $9,000 a year, and assuming you'll be able to earn 9 percent on the money you set aside.
- Another alternative would be to set aside $1,507; as college costs rise, so will your income and ability to increase your annual savings at the same inflation rate of 6 percent straight through to graduation.
- The most conservative approach would be to simply set aside $21,492 today. Based on these assumptions, you'd never have to invest another penny for your child's college education.

For parents with children opting for private colleges that can cost up to $20,000 per year today, the situation is even more serious.

- By the year 2011, an Ivy League undergraduate education could reach $235,597.
- This expense can be achieved using the same assumptions as above. By investing $5,590 annually so that by the time college started, you'd have enough to cover this cost.
- Invest $3,349 annually and increase this amount by the rate of inflation (6 percent) through to graduation.
- Or invest $47,760 today.

With numbers like these, it is clear that planning to meet educational needs is as essential as planning to meet housing and retirement costs.

The Price of Life

In the past, the Industrial Revolution set the stage for the average American worker to retire at age 65 due to the physical labor becoming increasingly more difficult. He consequently, lived approximately another seven years to age seventy-two. This made investing during the retirement years a little simpler than it is today, where the average worker may retire at age fifty-five and live thirty years or more. The average joint life expectancy of a couple, male age sixty and a female age fifty-seven, is twenty-two years. This places a burden on their accumulated assets and ability to generate sufficient income to support their lifestyle, net of taxes and inflation. There are four principal sources of retirement funds.

- Social Security
- Company Pension

- Money Earned
- Money Inherited

In 1950 Social Security supported one retired person for every thirty still working. Today there are three people working to fund one retired individual. It is projected that thirty years from now, for every two people working, one will be retired. This doesn't provide a great deal of comfort as to whether Social Security can generate meaningful income in the future. In the upside-down business world today, with mergers and acquisitions, as well as companies failing, no one can absolutely depend on a company pension to be there in the future. The ability to continue earning money, or to inherit it, is certainly variable at best.

50 and Out

It is an unfortunate travesty that in the greatest country in the world, the average savings of a fifty year-old couple is $2,500 which can barely buy a nice vacation, let alone a happy retirement. It may be necessary for these individuals to continue their lifestyle for, potentially, twenty to thirty years, net of taxes and inflation. You may need as much as 80 percent of your working income after retirement.

A million dollars is not worth what it used to be. You would need nearly $3.9 million today to have the same purchasing power in 1970 dollars net of inflation. A $1,000,000 investment generates $60,000 per year of income at a 6 percent withdrawal rate. The same $1,000,000 adjusted for 5 percent inflation, will be worth.

- $598,736 in 10 years - 6 percent withdrawal = $35,924 income per year

- $463,290 in 15 years - 6 percent withdrawal = $27,797 income per year
- $358,484 in 20 years - 6 percent withdrawal = $21,506 income per year
- $277,388 in 25 years - 6 percent withdrawal = $16,643 income per year

Income needed per year for retirement starting at a level of $60,000 based on a 5 percent inflation rate to maintain the same standard of living will require

- $97,734 in 10 years
- $124,736 in 15 years
- $159,198 in 20 years
- $203,181 in 25 years

The next chart illustrates how long your nest egg will last, showing an initial rate of withdrawal, as compared to the percentage rate of return, and the number of years it will take to deplete your savings or investment.

INITIAL RATE OF WITHDRAWAL	PERCENTAGE RATE OF RETURN				
	5%	6%	8%	9%	10%
25%	5	5	5	5	5
20%	6	6	6	6	7
19%	6	6	7	7	7
16%	7	7	8	8	9
15%	7	8	8	9	9
13%	9	9	10	10	11
11%	10	11	12	13	13
10%	11	12	13	14	15
8%	14	15	17	19	22
6%	18	20	25		
5%	21	24			
4%	27				

Social Security was never meant to support retirement, it was designed to augment other retirement income. The notion that we should be able to live on Social Security has, and will continue to be, eroded by the effects of inflation. Inflation has averaged 6 percent over the last twenty years and nearly 4 percent over the past ten years. At 6 percent inflation, your cost of living will double every twelve years; and yet there have been certain consumer items which have experienced more than 6 percent inflation. For example, the new Ford Mustang made its debut April 17, 1964, at $2,368. Assuming a 6 percent inflation, we should be able to buy a new Mustang today for $13,601. Yet, the '94 Mustang GT ranges from $17,755 to $27,000.

The Early Bird...

One of the basic fundamental disciplines of successful investing is to invest as early and as often as you can. The following chart illustrates a $5,000 investment for ten years only from age thirty-five, forty-five and age fifty-five, at an assumed (hypothetical) growth rate of 9 percent per year through age sixty-five. This confirms the fact that the earlier you begin an investment program, time and compound interest works in your favor.

AGE	35	45	55
35	$5,000		
36	$5,000		
37	$5,000		
38	$5,000		
39	$5,000		
40	$5,000		
41	$5,000		
42	$5,000		
43	$5,000		
44	$5,000		
45		$5,000	
46		$5,000	
47		$5,000	
48		$5,000	
49		$5,000	
50		$5,000	
51		$5,000	
52		$5,000	
53		$5,000	
54		$5,000	
55			$5,000
56			$5,000
57			$5,000
58			$5,000
59			$5,000
60			$5,000
61			$5,000
62			$5,000
63			$5,000
64			$5,000
TOTAL	$505,818	$213,663	$90,254

Wall Street Wallflower

Would you invest in the stock market if you knew?

- The prime rate would reach 21%
- Inflation would hit 16%
- There would be more bank and S&L failures since the depression
- The stock market would drop 508 points in a single day
- The president of the United States would be shot
- The U.S. would engage in an all out war in the Middle East

As earlier indicated, there have always been and always will be reasons not to invest in the stock market. In the past, we have experienced all types of political and economic events; yet, the only thing I know for sure is that the future will continue to change—and change creates opportunity. You want to wait until things seem a little cheaper. The newspaper headlines dramatize the short-term mentality of the average investor and the media in their approach to the stock market. Remarks like, investors await inflation news, or interest rate news, etc. My question is, who is going to remember this particular day one month, six months, or five years from now? We need to distance ourselves from this type of short term reporting of the news. A remark like "Market Plummets 20 Points" is misleading, I would not paraphrase a 20 point decline in the Dow at 3,500 as plummeting. However, this is an example of a typical headline to create interest in a story that may not be a story at all. Remember, the news media, like gossip, feeds on bad, not good, news.

Good News, Bad News

In 1982, when the Dow Jones Industrial Average hovered in the 780 range during a major recession, there was little positive news around to buy into. The old adage "buying on bad news and selling on good news" has always been hard to do. When the Dow increased to 1,200, an all time historic new level, after having increased 50 percent, it seemed expensive relative to where it was. At 2,400, after it doubled again, it seemed even more expensive. Then the 1987 correction of 508 points in a single day occurred, reminding everyone you can't take the market for granted. When John Templeton predicted 3,000, this in the early 1980s, it seemed an unattainable level. For the Dow to reach 5,000 by the year 2000, it will have to rise 5 percent per year (half the 10 percent average annual return since 1928). This could happen, but you should clearly expect breath-taking ups and downs along the way.

At each of these intervals, and certainly today is no exception, the market seems expensive (high) in historic terms. Dealing with this perception requires following three basic rules, all of them based on discipline.

- Discipline may be boring, but with all the exotics existing in the market today, most of us do best starting with, and sticking to, the basics. Discipline can also eliminate the need of trying to predict the future. This is an impossible task, particularly if you are talking about the stock market.
- The smartest investment program is one you start early and stay with.
- Focus on long-term goals, rather than the current Wall Street fad. Why? Because time is on your side. As indicated consistently throughout this book, time has proven to be a powerful investment ally.

Riding the Rollercoaster

A program of regular periodic investment through a time-honored investment strategy, called "dollar cost averaging," may provide you with the ability to smooth out the effects of short-term market fluctuations, as indicated in the chart below. Dollar cost averaging involves continuous investment in securities regardless of fluctuating price levels of the securities. The investor should also consider his financial ability to continue purchases through all market periods. View the following chart by investing $100 dollars from top to bottom down the left side and $100 dollars each time from bottom to top on the right side of the chart.

DOLLAR COST AVERAGING

INVEST	SHARES	PRICE	SHARES	INVEST
$100	1	$100	1	$100
$100	2	$50	2	$100
$100	4	$25	4	$100
$100	10	$10		

Your total investment of $100 seven different times ($700) at various prices, never exceeding your original cost, provides an average price per share of $29. Dollar cost averaging does not assure a profit nor protects against loss in declining markets.

A disciplined, systematic planned investment program of this type can provide an effective cost-efficient way to work toward your goal. It is impossible to consistently guess which way the market is headed. Even professional money managers, with all their access to technical data about the market, do not guess right all the time. Use your best judgment based on information from a reliable, reputable source, then stay with it—don't try to time the market's ups and downs by moving in and out of one investment after another. Disciplined investing isn't always interesting or exciting, but it can be effective.

Sitting on the Sideline

The S&P 500 (Standard & Poors Industrial Average consisting of 400 financial and 100 industrial and transportation stocks) averaged a 26.3 percent annualized rate of return during the time of the 1982 to 1987 bull market (1276 days). The following illustrates the penalty of missing the best days by sitting on the sideline and the adverse effects of attempting to time the market.

- 10 best days, 18.3 percent
- 20 best days, 13.1 percent
- 30 best days, 8.5 percent
- 40 best days, 4.3 percent

It is important you embrace a long-term investment approach and avoid the knee-jerk decision to run to safety each time a stock market correction occurs. Studies show a market-timer must be correct 70 to 80 percent of the time to make a profit. If you invested in the S&P 500 once each year over the last twenty years, on the very best day (when the market reached its low) compared to the very worst day (when the market reached its high), the difference in your rate of return would have only been 1.7 percent. This example is hypothetical and does not reflect the performance of any specific product. Investors may not invest directly in the S&P 500 index and the past performance of the index is no indication of future results. It is more important to invest when you have the money, as often and as early as you can, rather than trying to determine market highs and lows.

The problem is not knowing when one of these meaningful months or days will happen. Mondays are, historically, the biggest down days in the stock market. This is because, over the weekend, someone reads in a newspaper about an overdue market decline, creating sell orders on Monday. Why people are more prone to invest after the market gains 600 points and avoid the market after it drops 600 points is not logical, but that's what a lot of investors do. The two most recent corrections of 20 percent or more occurred in 1990 and 1987, indicated in the following chart.

MARKET CORRECTIONS

DATES OF CORRECTIONS		DECLINE	DAYS
MAY 29, 1946	MAY 17, 1947	23.2%	353
APRIL 6, 1956	OCT. 22, 1957	19.4%	564
DEC. 13, 1961	JUNE 26, 1962	27.1%	195
FEB. 9, 1966	OCT. 7. 1966	25.2%	24
DEC. 3, 1968	MAY 26, 1970	35.9%	539
JAN. 11, 1973	DEC. 6, 1974	45.1%	694
SEPT. 21, 1976	FEB. 28, 1978	26.9%	525
APRIL 27, 1981	AUG. 12, 1983	24.1%	472
AUG. 25, 1987	OCT. 19, 1987	36.1%	55
JULY 16, 1990	OCT. 11, 1990	21.2%	87

The 21.2 percent correction in 1990 and the 36.1 percent correction in 1987 were, I feel, aberrations representing severe short-term spikes in the market. Their duration only lasted eighty-seven and fifty-five days, respectively. If you look at other corrections since World War II, with similar percentage declines, the number of days these corrections lasted was much longer. You should anticipate corrections in the future not to be similar to 1987 and 1990, but consistent with historic corrections longer in duration.

Over the past sixty-five years the stock market has had fourteen up markets and thirteen down markets. You might feel that the odds of 50/50 are not particularly good. A further look at that statistic, however, shows:

- Since 1926, the average up market lasted 3.3 years and doubled investor's capital each time.

- The average down market lasted 1.5 years, losing 17 percent of investment capital.

Since 1945, the longest it has ever taken for the stock market (counting dividends) to fully recover from a period of losses was 3.5 years in the early 1970s. (The performance data quoted represents past performance only and is not indicative of future results.)

During the last century, the stock market has dropped 10 percent fifty times. Of those fifty declines, fifteen have averaged approximately 33 percent. Therefore, you might anticipate a 10 percent correction on the average of every two years, and a correction in excess of 30 percent every six or seven years when investing in equities. These percentages coincide with prior declines in the market since World War II. A 10 percent correction in the Dow at the 3,700 range equals 370 points, significant but as a percentage of the total, not major. A 33 percent correction of a 3,700 Dow equals 1,222 points, a major correction by anyone's definition, and one that could clearly last longer than corrections in 1987 and 1990.

If you don't believe in corrections, consider the Japanese stock market (Nikkei) which fell 63 percent from its high of nearly 39,000 at the end of 1989, to 14,309 in August of 1992. Market corrections are a natural part of the cycle. Peter Sellers personified this in the movie "Being There," when his character likened the economy to a garden. The economic prosperity of summer is followed by the recession of fall and the dormant period of winter. This is followed by the economic rebirth of spring into the growth of a new summer. The stock market, like life, is a state of mind.

Investors who lost money in the 1987 correction (when the market fell 508 points in a single day) were those who panicked and ran to the sidelines to secure their losses by selling. The patient investors who remained in the market, or dollar cost averaged over the long run, generally did well. Everyone always seems to have an opinion about where the market is going. If you get caught in the emotions of these corrections and try to sit out the market corrections, you are likely to miss some of the good days. One way you can deal with some of the short term instability is through diversification.

Diversification

While market corrections naturally occur, money managers can also experience corrections within their portfolio as they make adjustments and position themselves from different segments of the market to others. Short-term poor performance by an otherwise efficient and sound fundamental manager with an excellent track record should not be abandoned. Poor performance after a quarter or two, or even a year, unless there has been some fundamental change in philosophy, discipline, or management, should not prompt you to sell that fund.

How can you tell if the returns received on an investment determine the risk involved? There are several technical methods to help. However, like most technical or scientific methods, they aren't foolproof. Portfolio managers use Alpha and Beta to qualify risk and return, and the modern portfolio theory to compare specific investments for risk and reward. Beta measures an investment risk against the overall market. The S&P 500 has been assigned a Beta of one. Therefore, investment with a Beta of two is twice as volatile as the overall market. An investor would then expect this investment to correspondingly out-perform the market. However, the rating is never to be considered a guarantee.

Alpha is the difference between what an investment actually returns and its Beta. If an investment returns more than its expected return, it would have a positive Alpha. If the Alpha is negative, the return does not justify the risk. This information is routinely provided by many publishers of mutual fund data.

Owning individual stocks can be profitable or hazardous to your financial future. A stock declining from $175 to $51 or $50 to $5 can be devastating, even if you dollar cost average. If you choose to purchase individual stocks, a guideline may be owning a minimum of 500 shares of no fewer than twelve stocks. This will help provide reasonable diversification and, hopefully, affords sufficient benefit if a stock increases to make it worth the risk. If your average stock price is $20 X 500 shares X 12 stocks = $120,000. If you don't have this amount of money, an alternative to the market may be mutual funds that generally provide greater diversification with less individual market risk.

When a stock loses 50 percent of its value, it has to increase 100 percent to return to its original price. Dollar cost averaging may help in situations like this but may not insure you'll recover your loss and achieve appreciation beyond where you started. One of the obvious advantages of mutual funds is not only the professional management, but a diversified portfolio which may include hundreds of stocks in several dozen industries providing exposure to a larger number of issues than a normal investor could purchase. This consequently, reduces the risk by broadening your participation to a greater number of markets and stocks.

It is equally important to select a variety of mutual funds and to diversify management style, discipline, and capitalization. From time to time, growth funds (growth managers or investors believe they can see the future more clearly by choosing stocks with greater future potential earnings) may be more in favor on Wall Street. Other times, value funds (value managers or investors are much less dependent on what they can see as growth potential far into the future but rather look for stocks that are undervalued) will be more in favor. Diversify your portfolio using the style box to determine a fund's investment objectives.

Additional consideration is given to market capitalization which shows the size of a company in which a fund invests.

- Small (funds with market capitalization's less than $1 billion)
- Medium (market capitalization's between $1 and $5 billion)
- Large (market capitalization greater than $5 billion)

Growth, value or blended styles of management may be selected to best suit your view of the market. The following stock style box indicates a blended (combination of value and growth) large cap manager.

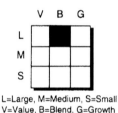

L=Large, M=Medium, S=Small
V=Value, B=Blend, G=Growth

Picking suitable investment objectives are important. This asset allocation process (diversifying your money into different categories) may include setting your goals and objectives for a balanced portfolio, as the following suggests.

1. Determine Appropriate Allocation
   - Equities
   - Fixed Income
   - Cash

2. Select Appropriate Management Style
   - Growth
   - Value
   - Blend

3. Select Appropriate Capitalization
   • Small Stocks
   • Medium Stocks
   • Large Stocks

4. Select Appropriate Investment Discipline
   • Aggressive Growth
   • Growth and Income
   • International Growth
   • Equity Income

5. Select Appropriate Mutual Funds
   • Fund A
   • Fund B
   • Fund C, etc.

Global Growth

A discussion of diversification should also include the international opportunities for U.S. investors. In 1973 non-U.S. companies represented only 39 percent of the world stock market. In 1993 they represented 63 percent of the market, which included:

• Ten of the ten largest construction companies
• Ten of the ten largest banking companies
• Eight of the ten largest chemical companies
• Eight of the ten largest machinery and engineering companies
• Seven of the ten largest automobile companies

Non-U.S. companies may account for 88 percent of the world's stock market size in less than ten years, if current trends continue.

The largest potential growth for world economies is China. With 1.2 billion people, it currently represents the third largest economy after the U.S. and Japan. In China there are thirty-two people for every television compared to one television for every person in the U.S. In Beijing City alone, there are twelve million people, seven million bicycles, and 70,000 automobiles. As we near the turn of the millennium, the global economy of the next century will provide immeasurable opportunities from the following developing areas: the Asia Pacific region of Hong Kong and Korea, Taiwan and Singapore; the Four Tiger countries of Malaysia, Philippines, Indonesia, and Thailand; and the Latin American and Central American countries. Areas such as Vietnam, since the U.S. lifted the nineteen-year economic embargo, and India are additional considerations. Since 1992 the continual expansion of the European Community has opened a single market of 350 million people.

As U.S. markets shrink, as part of the world's capitalization, the performance of international markets becomes increasingly more important. It is, however, necessary to note that investments outside the U.S., especially in developing countries, are subject to additional risk. These include currency fluctuations, political and social instability, differing security regulations and accounting standards, limited public information, possible changes in the taxation, and periods of liquidity.

World stock market performance during the past ten years finds the U.S. domestic equities market closer to the bottom in performance, rather than the top. If you purchase global mutual funds, you may not own as many international equities as you think. International funds only hold foreign stocks while global equities can, and usually do, hold U.S. equities. During the period January 1973 to December 1992, a portfolio consisting of 50 percent U.S. stocks (S&P 500 Index) and 50 percent invested in foreign stocks (Morgan Stanley Index) produced the highest returns and least risk. Investors, however, cannot invest directly in the S&P 500

Index; and the past performance of the index is not an indication of future results or the future performance of any product.

Summary

- Speculating is gambling, always use fundamentally sound investments.
- Ignore stock tips and proprietary information, it's called inside information and it's illegal.
- Minimize leverage and avoid debt when possible. It's difficult to work from a position of strength if you're in debt.
- Invest when you have the money, and as early, and as often as you can.
- Diversify your portfolio.
- Don't look for a reason not to invest because you will always find one.
- Don't run for the exit lights every time the market gets nervous.
- Don't get discouraged.
- Expect the market to go down, because it will.
- Dollar cost average your investment when it does.
- The best results occur long term.
- Understand compound interest, inflation and, taxes and the effect they will have on your investments.
- Avoid emotional decisions.

Act now, save more, and invest better. I hope these principles help you achieve a greater balance to your financial matters, as they have guided me to financial security.

Chapter Five

Fit for Life

*"Your choice of diet can influence your
long-term prospects more than any other
action you might take."*
—former Surgeon General C. Everett Koop

All the money in the world cannot buy your health. There are a lot of wealthy people who would give it all up to regain their fitness. This chapter discusses how our diets affect our well-being, and what we can do to avoid many illnesses. As wonderful as the medical profession is in this country, and with all the incredible advances in technology, most of the medical profession is oriented toward the treatment and cure of disease, not the prevention. Of the nation's 125 medical schools, only thirty have a required course in nutrition. As indicated by a recent Senate investigation, the average physician receives less than three hours of nutrition training during four years of medical school.

Great Expectations

Mounting evidence shows there is no reason to expect, or settle for, higher blood pressure, loss of mobility, increased weight, and a continually compromised lifestyle as we get older. These acceptable myths in our society are a tragic commentary on what we have come to expect of ourselves and older generations.

A large portion of the U.S. population is overweight and continues to diet unsuccessfully. Take a look at your stomach, it may be a reflection of the condition of your heart. The Journal of the American Medical Association suggests there are increased health risks for obesity. After analyzing the health of 19,297 male Harvard alumni from 1962 to 1966, researchers found those weighing the least were less likely to die over the next three decades. A complex formula, taking into account both height and weight, divided these men into five categories. This study showed that as body mass increased, so did the risk of death. The most overweight men were found to have as much as 67 percent higher risk of dying at a younger age. Men considered heaviest were those weighing in excess of 181 pounds with a height of 5'10". These men were also found to have a two and a half times greater risk of heart disease.

An effective way to deal with these issues is a regimen of changing what you eat preferable to a low fat, high fiber diet accompanied by moderate exercise. This enables you to maintain a proper weight without regaining lost weight, which can lead to a healthier, happier, more productive individual. Researchers at Harvard University and the New England Medical Center in Boston found after a seven-year study that obese women complete about one-third less years of schooling, are 20 percent less likely to marry, and earn a yearly average of $6,710 less than their slimmer counterparts. To make this worse, more than 50 million Americans who are overweight will spend $32 billion on dieting this year alone. Conversely, overweight men are 11 percent less likely to marry than thinner men but are only slightly affected financially. Now let's discuss how the cause and effect of our diet relates to our health.

Where's the Meat?

There are those who argue that we need animal products to be healthy. The word "vegetarian" comes from the Latin *vegetus* meaning "vigorous and alive." To dispel the notion that large mammals, like ourselves, require meat to be healthy, one only needs to think of the elephant or horse who performs great feats of strength, yet feeds entirely on plant food. There is evidence that human bodies tend toward vegetarianism, instead of being flesh-eaters. Normal human intestines are twelve times longer than our body length. The normal length of those of a carnivorous animal is only three times its body length. Our teeth are comprised of mostly molars, which are more appropriate for chewing grains and vegetables than the pointed canine teeth other animals use to rip and tear flesh. Our skin is made up of millions of pores. Carnivorous animals do not have pores. Dogs, for example, eliminate heat from their tongue, nose, and pads of their feet. Our fingernails are flat, in contrast to claws. Our salivary glands are well-developed. We have smooth tongues and mammary glands, all of which are more vegetarian characteristics.

Many individuals throughout history who have made a difference were vegetarians:

- George Bernard Shaw
- Leonardo DaVinci
- Ralph Waldo Emerson
- Henry David Thoreau
- Benjamin Franklin
- Mahatma Gandhi
- Albert Schweitzer
- Sir Isaac Newton
- Albert Einstein

It is a misconception that society has always been a meat-based culture. It is only the twentieth century technology of mass-slaughtering animals that brought meat to the table of the average wage earner. The following diseases and conditions can be prevented, or substantially improved (sometimes even cured), with a low-fat, high-fiber diet, free from animal products: strokes, heart disease, prostate cancer, breast cancer, colon cancer, hypertension, osteoporosis, hypoglycemia, obesity, diabetes, hemorrhoids, diverticulitis, peptic ulcers, asthma, constipation and gall stones.

The American Heart Association, the National Cancer Institute, and many other health authorities recommend we consume no more than 30 percent of our calories from fat. Although the average American diet consists of 40 to 50 percent of calories from fat, it simply consists of too much and the wrong kind. Fat is not bad, in proper amounts. It's required for maintaining proper health. The fact is, our bodies do not require any saturated fats and could maintain proper health with just 10 percent of our calories from unsaturated fat. The average person eating 2,000 calories per day should consume no more than 65 grams (2000 x 30% ÷ 9 = 65) of fat. To convert grams of fat to teaspoons, divide the total fat by 4 (65 ÷ 4 = 16 teaspoons of fat).

The Diet Downfall

Diets do not work if you do not change your activity level and what you eat. You have to change your metabolism by becoming fit. Only muscle burns fat. Almost everyone gains back the weight they lost, plus more. The reason for this is the body goes into a starvation mode, anticipating a reduction in calorie intake. It then begins defensively storing calories in the form of fat. The only way to fully lose weight is to change what you eat and moderately exercise. Dieting has very little to do with *how much* you eat, but rather *what* you eat, especially your fat intake. The benefit of exercise includes reduction in body fat, an increase in muscle mass (being physically fit), lower blood pressure, and blood cholesterol. Your ability to lose weight and maintain an ideal weight has a lot to do with your metabolism, the body's ability to burn calories at rest. Fat does not burn calories at rest, while muscle continually burns calories. Therefore, an overweight person who skips breakfast and lunch, then overeats at dinner and goes to sleep soon afterward, should realize those calories are stored as fat, with little ability to burn calories. Conversely, using the same scenario, a person consuming a larger portion of their calories earlier in the day from breakfast and lunch sleeps with fewer calories to burn at rest. Also, a person with greater muscle mass developed from exercise consequently lowers body fat by burning calories at rest—even while they sleep.

The following examples illustrate how a fast food (high-fat, low fiber) diet compares to a vegetarian (low-fat, high-fiber) diet. The summaries clearly speak for themselves. The chart below contains 133 grams of fat, equal to ingesting 33 teaspoons of fat ($133 \div 4 = 33$).

	Serv	Cal	Total Fat Grams	Satur Fat Grams	Chol Mgs	Protein Grams	Carbo Grams	Fiber Grams	Sodium Mgs
BREAKFAST									
No Meal									
LUNCH									
Burger King DBL Whopper W/CH	1	950	63	24	195	52	47	3	1340
Fries (Med)	1	400	20	5	0	5	43	3	240
Coke 22 oz.	1	260					70		15
DINNER									
Taco Bell Burrito Supreme (Beef)	2	1050	50	22	144	50	N/A	N/A	2836
Coke 21 oz.	1	210					55		20
TOTAL		2870	133	51	339	107	215	6	4451

	Serv	Cal	Total Fat Grams	Satur Fat Grams	Chol Mgs	Protein Grams	Carbo Grams	Fiber Grams	Sodium Mgs
Recommended Guidelines			10 to 30%	<10% of cal	<300 mgs	12-15% of cal	55-58% of cal	20-30 gms	1800 to 2400 mgs
Actual			42.7%	16.4%	339	15.2%	30.1%	6	247%
High/Low			H	H	H		L	L	H

To lose one pound, you must burn at least 3,500 calories more than you consume.

	Serv	Cal	Total Fat Grams	Satur Fat Grams	Chol Mgs	Protein Grams	Carbo Grams	Fiber Grams	Sodium Mgs
BREAKFAST									
No Meal									
LUNCH									
McDonald's ¼lb. W/CH	1	490	27.0	10.0	115	28.0	36.0	2.0	1090
Fries (Lrg)	1	400	22.0	5.0		6.0	46.0	4.0	200
Coke 32 oz.	1	300					82.0		30
DINNER									
Domino's Pizza Dbl ch, pepp	4	1341	66.2	26.6	108	59.2	127.4	6.4	3016
Coke 21 oz.	1	210					55.0		20
TOTAL		2741	115.2	41.6	223	93.2	346.4	12.4	4356
Recommended Guidelines			10 to 30%	<10% of cal	<300 mgs	12-15% of cal	55-58% of cal	20-30 gms	1800 to 2400 mgs
Actual			37.8%	13.7%	223	13.6%	50.6%	12.4	242%
High/Low			H	H			L	L	H

Many adults frequently consume similar meals, mostly out of convenience and often subject their children to the same. The convenience of fast food in this country has substantially contributed to the deterioration of health in our society.

If you also add a lifestyle of inactivity, due to a growing business career, to this scenario, it causes increased weight gain which is another contributing risk factor. It is not unusual for many people to have coffee or coke, a cigarette and a doughnut or skip breakfast altogether. The day's most important meal, and consume more than 40 percent of their total calories from fat, instead of the recommended 10 to 20 percent.

The following chart shows a healthier alternative. Confirming that dieting and proper weight maintenance have less to do with how much you eat but rather what you eat. Notice how much more food you can eat on this type of diet.

	Serv	Cal	Total Fat Grams	Satur Fat Grams	Chol Mgs	Protein Grams	Carbo Grams	Fiber Grams	Sodium Mgs
BREAKFAST									
Oatmeal	1	145	2.4	0.4		6.0	25.2	0.4	1.0
Orange Juice 12 oz.	1	166	0.8	<0.2		2.6	38.6	0.4	4.0
LUNCH									
Lima Bean Potato Plate w/rice	1	212.9	4.1	0.7		7.5	40.6	6.3	6.6
Caesar Salad w/o egg yolk	1	93.8	9.3	1.4	3.0	1.2	2.2	0.7	81.1
Banana & Oranges-juiced	1&2	228	1.0	<0.3		3.6	57.5	8.0	1.0
Carrot Juice	5	155	0.5	<0.5		3.5	36.5	11.5	125.0
DINNER									
Pasta/Marinara low fat parmesan	2	480	3.0		5.0	20.0	96.0	N/A	430.0
Grapefruit	1	92	0.2	<0.2		1.2	23.8	0.6	<2.0
Pita Bread	2	300	4.0	N/A		12.0	56.0	1.4	640.0
Salad No Fat Dressing	1	95	0.5	<0.5		2.7	20.7	2.7	429.0
Tapioca Pudding No Fat	2	200				4.0	44.0	N/A	380.0
TOTAL		2168	25.8	4.2	8.0	64.3	441.1	32.0	2099.7
Recommended Guidelines			10 to 30%	<10% of cal	<300 mgs	12-15% of cal	55-58% of cal	20-30 gms	1800 to 2400 mgs
Actual			10.7%	1.7%	8.0	11.9%	81.4%	32	116.6%

Label Library

Packaging and labeling for the food industry has left many consumers in a dilemma when trying to choose a lower-fat diet. In
many cases, labels do not clarify exactly what you are buying.
Recent legislative changes requiring products to be labeled using
a 2,000 and 2,500 calorie daily diet is even more confusing to the
consumer. If you do not fall into one of these categories, it's
harder to figure out your proper levels.

The most important formulas you need to know in determining fat content is explained below. This formula will help you
calculate the percentage of fat calories in a food product. There
are nine calories in a gram of fat, the formula is:

Grams of Fat per Serving x 9
Total Fat Grams per Serving ÷ Total Calories per Serving
The Answer Gives You the Total Percentage of Calories From Fat

Here's how to calculate it: 16 grams of fat per serving x 9 calories per gram = 144 calories ÷ 200 total calories = 72 percent.
Be careful with products that claim, for example, to be 98 percent
fat free. A product 98 percent fat free can still have 27 percent of
its calories from fat. If the product contains 100 calories and 3
grams of fat (3 x 9 = 27 ÷ 100 = 27 percent).

The Weight War

Determine your desirable weight in pounds and multiply by 10 to
12. The answer equals the average number of calories per day
required by a sedentary person to maintain each pound of body
weight. **Do not reduce your caloric intake under 1,200 calories
per day without first consulting a physician. If you are pregnant,
nursing, have any health problems or are under the age of eigh-**

teen, consult a physician before starting any diet. **Do not lose more than two pounds per week after the first week. Very rapid weight loss may cause health problems.** A moderately active person should multiply their desired weight by 12 to 15, an extremely active individual by 15 to 18, to arrive at the amount of daily calories required to maintain his or her resting metabolism (basal metabolic rate equals calories to sustain current body weight). Your requirements may be higher or lower within these ranges.

Desirable body weight x 10 =
calories required for sedentary people
Desirable body weight x 12 =
calories required for moderately active people
Desirable body weight x 15 =
calories required for active people

If you currently weigh 200 pounds and would like to reach a more ideal weight of 170 pounds, multiply 170 x 12 and begin a moderate exercise program. This means you need 2,040 calories to reach and maintain 170 pounds. Any caloric intake above or below this number will generate proportionate weight gain or loss. Always keep in mind that this formula is also influenced by age. As you become older, your caloric requirements generally decrease. Consider these other factors:

- Sex: Men may require more calories than women.
- Activity Level: Physically active people burn and require more calories.
- Body Composition: A physically fit individual burns more calories than someone who is overweight and out of shape.
- Genetics: Can play a role in your tendency to weight gain.

Here is an example for a woman who wants to weigh 125 pounds

Weight 125 x 12 (moderately active) = 1,500
1,500 Maximum Calories to Achieve Desired Weight
Total Calories 1,500 x 30 percent =
450 (Maximum Calories from Fat)
450 Calories From Fat ÷ 9 =
50 (1 Calorie has 9 Grams of Fat)
50 Allowable Grams of Total Fat Per Day
1,500 Calories x 10 percent Saturated Fat
150 Total Saturated Fat Calories Per Day
150 ÷ 9 = 16.6 Total Grams of Saturated Fat Per Day

Fat is only one aspect of the total plan to be healthy. Other nutritional requirements include proper levels of protein and complex carbohydrates.

Protein Power

Proteins are comprised of various amino acids and are necessary for proper feeding of every body cell. The body naturally manufactures some amino acids; however, nine are not produced by the body. Animal or vegetable protein must be consumed to get these nine essential amino acids. Animal protein, while considered complete and containing these additional amino acids, is high in fat and cholesterol when consumed in the form of meat, eggs, and dairy products. Conversely, plant protein sources are not considered complete because they do not contain all the necessary amino acids. They have to be eaten individually, or in combination with each other, to be complete. The good news is that protein from plant sources is usually low in fat and high in fiber. The combination of legumes and grains provide this complete protein structure. There are many people who feel they will not get enough protein without eating meat. Studies have found that about 54 grams of protein is sufficient for an average 150 pound adult.

- In fact, one study shows the average protein intake of male vegetarians (no animal products) to be 128 percent of the daily recommendation.
- Compared to 150 percent of lacto-ovo vegetarians (uses milk and eggs but no flesh products)
- Compared to 192 percent of non-vegetarians

These studies conclude that all are above the recommended amount of necessary protein intake.

You can determine your maximum recommended daily caloric protein by the following equation which provides your average grams of protein required daily as recommended by government guidelines.

(1 Pound = 2.2 Kilograms)
150 Pound Person ÷ 2.2 = 68 Kilograms
68 Kilograms x .8 =
54 Grams of Protein (.8 Grams Per Kilogram of Body Weight)
150 pound person x 12 moderate exerciser =
1,800 calories per day
1,800 calories x 13 percent =
234 protein calories (range 12 to 15 percent)
234 protein calories ÷ 4 = 58 grams of protein per day

Fueling the Tank

Complex carbohydrates are made of various starches and sugars that the body uses for energy, as well as the repair and building of tissue. These are found in plants, fruits, vegetables, and whole grains. Carbohydrates should provide up to 55 to 58 percent of your daily caloric intake. Refined or simple carbohydrates are found in highly processed foods, such as sugar, candy and cakes, and provide less nutritional value. Your daily caloric intake of refined carbohydrates should be kept under 10 percent. Protein and carbohydrates both contain four calories per gram.

170 pound person x 12 moderate exerciser =
2,040 calories per day (BMR)
2,040 calories per day x 58 percent =
1,183 complex carbohydrate calories
1,183 carbohydrates ÷ 4 =
296 grams of carbohydrates per day

The Wrong Stuff

The National Academy of Sciences recommends we consume no more than 1,800 milligrams of sodium per day. One teaspoon of salt contains about 2,000 milligrams of sodium. The average person needs only about 200 milligrams a day of sodium to function properly. Most Americans consume between 4,000 and 6,000 milligrams each day. It is estimated that 60 million Americans have high blood pressure (hypertension), which is a form of coronary heart disease. A high intake of sodium has been linked to this condition.

In 1951 the average intake of sugars, including corn syrup and refined sweeteners, was 110 pounds per person, and 136 pounds in 1990. To convert grams of sugar to teaspoons, divide by four. One 22 oz. Coke has 17 teaspoons of sugar.

Risky Business

The government suggests we consume no more than 300 grams of cholesterol per day. Although cholesterol is necessary for healthy body maintenance, you should note that our bodies produce a complete daily supply (approx. 1,000 milligrams). Consequently, it would be possible to eat a diet completely void of cholesterol without causing any deficiency to our system. The following are recommended guidelines for proper total blood cholesterol levels. Statistics show that for every one percent decrease in blood cholesterol, we can experience a 1 to 2 percent decline in heart disease risk.

- 200 or Higher Indicates High Risk
- 175 to 200 Indicates Acceptable Level
- 150 to 175 Indicates Low Level
- 150 or Below Indicates Low Risk

A proper diet consisting of a low-fat, low-cholesterol diet is essential. HDL (High Density Lipids), the good cholesterol, picks up circulating cholesterol from arteries and delivers it to the liver for metabolization. The following are recommended guidelines for HDL blood levels.

- 65 or higher Indicates Low Risk
- 35 to 65 Indicates Acceptable Risk
- 35 or below Indicates High Risk

To raise HDL levels without drugs requires a regular exercise program. Your ratio of total cholesterol to HDL cholesterol may be a better indicator of your risk of heart disease. Your ratio can be improved by raising your HDL or lowering your total cholesterol.

- A Ratio of 4.5 or Higher Indicates High Risk
- 3.5 to 4.5 Indicates Acceptable Risk
- 3.5 or Lower Indicates Low Risk

Triglycerides are the circulating fats in your blood. Affected by what you eat, they are associated in some people with an increased risk of coronary heart disease. Your level may be influenced by obesity, diabetes, stress, and other factors.

Your LDL (low density lipids) cholesterol is the bad type linked to the development of arterial blockage.

- 130 or Above Indicates Elevated Risk
- 100 to 130 Indicates Acceptable Level
- 100 or Lower Indicates Low Risk

Heart Disease—The Beat Goes On

Of the many illnesses that can be prevented, improved, or even cured by lifestyle changes, the largest killer in America is coronary heart disease. Two-thirds of all Americans will ultimately die of coronary heart disease. Every fifth man and every sixteenth woman will suffer a heart attack before age sixty. Five hundred thousand Americans will die this year of heart attacks—half of them before they can reach a hospital. The good news is that since 1968 the incidence of heart attacks has declined 25 percent, possibly due to a heightened awareness of these medical concerns and a diligent educational process undertaken by many responsible organizations. The bad news is that this often preventable disease continues to plague the American population.

The heart is the most important muscle in your body. It beats approximately 37 million times per year and is never given time to rest. The most recent figures indicate that 923,422 people die of heart and blood vessel diseases each year. Specifically, cardiac disease kills one person every minute in this country alone. Every minute someone suffers a stroke in this country, 27 percent die and 60 percent are impaired for life.

Not taking care of yourself will unmistakably cause poor health and cost you a lot of money. A recent federally sponsored study indicated the average cost of a stroke to be $15,000 a patient. The national cost of treatment and rehab is $30 billion per year, not considering loss of wages. This national study, coordinated by Duke University Medical Center, indicated about 550,000 people suffer a stroke each year and 150,000 die. According to the American Heart Association, smoking accounted for 20 percent of the deaths. Currently, heart disease comprises the largest portion of America's health care costs. Open heart surgeries cost $5 billion in 1984, compared to $50 billion in 1993. The cost of routine by-pass surgery today is $40,000.

My mother recently underwent quadruple by-pass surgery. For several days following the surgery, she was fed intravenously while in the intensive care unit. I was astounded to find the first day she was allowed solid food, she was served a breakfast that consisted of bacon, eggs, and sausage. I asked the attending ICU nurse why this would be the normal diet for patients in this situation. Her answer was, "I guess we have to keep business booming."

Studies of autopsies performed during the Vietnam war on young men in their twenties showed signs of advanced coronary heart disease. Considering the fast food diet of today's youth, the onset of heart disease will likely start occurring at even younger ages. An overwhelming 67 percent of all American children, ages 7 through 12, have three or more risk factors for coronary heart disease. We could save more than 100,000 lives per year by altering these risk factors. Risk factors for coronary artery disease include:

- Smoking
- High Blood Pressure
- Serum Cholesterol
- Obesity
- Stress
- Lack of Exercise
- Genetics or Family History
- Diabetes Mellitus

Many experts feel heart disease could be substantially reduced by altering type A behavior. Traditionally, a person with type A behavior (aggressive, stressed person) has a tendency toward smoking, obesity, inactivity, excessive drinking, and demonstrates other behavior patterns that can become risk factors.

Each year, three times as many men have heart attacks than women. Heart disease has always been considered a "male affliction," probably because men develop the problem at an earlier age (on average ten years earlier than women). Yet, women catch up after menopause. By age 65, one in three women have some form of heart disease. Eighty-seven thousand (87,000) American women die of stroke each year.

The risk of death from heart disease for the average American male is 50 percent. The risk of death from heart disease for an average male who consumes no meat is 15 percent. Risk of death from heart disease for the average male who consumes no meat, egg, or dairy products is 4 percent.

> *"I don't understand why asking people*
> *to eat a well-balanced, vegetarian, diet is*
> *considered drastic, while it is medically*
> *conservative to cut people open or put*
> *them on powerful cholesterol lowering*
> *drugs for the rest of their lives."*
> —Dean Ornish, MD

The Framingham Study

The well-known Framingham Study took place over a twenty-year period in the Massachusetts town of Framingham, twenty miles west of Boston. It studied the effects of weight, blood pressure, and serum cholesterol relative to coronary heart disease in men who were between forty-five and sixty-two years of age. The following chart illustrates the increased risk of coronary heart disease for a male, age forty-five with increased blood pressure and serum cholesterol.

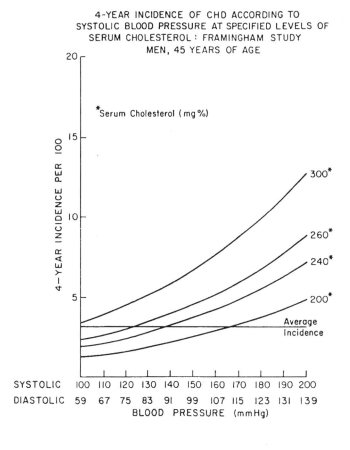

The evidence is overwhelming that a change in these risk factors can, and will, substantially reduce the risk of developing heart disease. Some actually believe you can reverse coronary heart disease even after its onset. However, it isn't clear whether an elevated serum cholesterol is as important a risk factor for heart disease for those over the age of seventy as it is in middle-aged men.

The Big "C"

Throughout the world, a high-fat, low-fiber diet correlates to an increased risk of breast cancer, which in 1994 alone killed 46,000 American women. Population studies have repeatedly shown the correlation between dietary fat and the occurrence of cancer in several parts of the body, especially the breasts, prostate, and large bowel.

The news about cancer prevention is getting better all the time. It is suggested that 80 percent of all cancers are related to the environment and diet rather than factors we cannot control, such as heredity. If you change the things you can control, there is strong evidence you may reduce your risk, and your family's risk, of developing cancer. Thirty-five percent of all cancer deaths may be related to what we eat. Conversely, a diet low in fat and high in fiber, including fruits, vegetables and whole grains, may reduce your cancer risk. A recent study indicated that a high-fat diet increases six times the average American's risk of developing lung cancer. According to one of these studies, red meat represented the food group with the strongest association with cancer.

"American fast food diets and the meat eating habits of the wealthy around the world support a food system that diverts food resources from the hungry. A diet higher in whole grains and legumes, and lower in beef and other meat, is not just healthier for ourselves, but also contributes to changing the world's system that feeds some people and leaves others hungry," says Dr. Waldon Bello, Executive Director, Institute for Food and Development Policy.

Wimping Out or Working Out

Exercise may not be fun until it becomes part of your life. Then you will not be able to imagine life without it. Remember you either have time to work out now or time to be sick later.

An on-going study has tracked the health and lifestyles of 16,936 Harvard alumni. Researchers have found lower death rates in all age groups as physical activity increased. Men who burned 2,000 calories or more per week had a 28 percent lower death rate at younger ages than men who exercise less, or not at all.

The importance of exercise is that it becomes a habit and part of your weekly routine. Remember, it takes twenty-one days to break an old habit or develop a new one. It is equally important to find a workout you enjoy doing; otherwise, you will not continue to exercise. While moderate exercise shows the greatest improvement relative to reduction in coronary heart disease, selecting an exercise which is the least stressful to the body is also helpful. This exercise may simply be walking. You can generate just as much aerobic benefit from walking as running; you just have to do it twice as long. The only difference between jogging or walking for ten minutes is ten calories.

One of the great highs in life is experiencing your body functioning the way it was meant to function. Exercising pumps endorphins into your system, alleviates stress and aches, and clears your mind as your legs work like pistons pumping oxygen-enriched blood to your brain and circulatory system. This gives you an incredible feeling of well-being and euphoria, proving life can be a state of mind. This is the way it's supposed to be. Search out these rewards instead of addictions like cigarettes, caffeine, alcohol, prescription or illegal drugs. Some of my best ideas have come to me at these times. If you haven't experienced these feelings, you're missing some great moments. It is extremely important to consult your doctor before beginning any exercise program, to establish a baseline of your medical condition, as well as to determine whether you are physically able to undertake the program of your choice.

Reach for the Stars

Stretching before any physical activity is very important. It allows your muscles to loosen up and become warm. Muscles can stretch as much as 20 percent, causing greater elasticity, flexibility, and lessening the possibility of injury. There are many excellent books published that cover a variety of stretching and warm-up exercises. Stretching simply feels good and can have an incredible effect on your physical well being. Stretching should be done before and after your aerobic activity. Breathing properly is equally important. When was the last time you took a deep breath and exhaled all the stale air from the bottom of your lungs? Take a half dozen deep breaths and fill your lungs with fresh oxygen. This oxygenates your body and clears your head. You'll feel better immediately. By becoming shallow breathers, people are not maximizing the benefits of deep breathing—most notably the rejuvenation of body and mind.

Target Zone

The standard method of determining your target zone and maximum heart rate can be found by subtracting your age from 220 and multiplying that number by 65 to 80 percent. My target zone is at least 112 heart beats per minute but not more than 138.

EXAMPLE: 220 - 47 (MY AGE) = 173 x 80% = 138 =
MAX. HEART RATE
220 - 47 = 173 x 65% = 112 = MIN. HEART RATE

However, to determine the correct intensity level of your workout you should:

- Be able to carry on a normal conversation without being out of breath. If you can't, you are probably working too hard.
- If your muscles fatigue, slow down your pace.
- If you cannot continue your pace for more than a few minutes, slow down.
- Work hard enough to challenge yourself without pushing yourself to exhaustion.

Doing aerobic exercises that reach your target zone, twenty to forty minutes, three to five times a week, is all you need to stay in good aerobic condition.

Pumping Iron

In addition to aerobic training, an excellent way to keep your body in good shape and properly toned, at any age, is with weight training. Look at some of the weight trainers in their forties like Frank Zane, Mr. Olympia 1977-1978-1979; and in their fifties, Larry Scott, Mr. Olympia 1965-1966; and even their sixties, like Albert Beckles. All remain in incredible shape. Appropriate weight training can be beneficial at any age to build muscle mass and bone density. A stronger body reduces the risk of falls and injuries. Average bone loss of a sixty-five-year-old female meat-eater is 35 percent compared to a vegetarian of 18 percent.

Given a choice, most women would not want to lose one third of their skeletal structure by the age of sixty-five.

There's no reason to expect physical deterioration as you get older. At age forty-seven, fifty-seven or sixty-seven you can have a better body and more energy than many younger people. At any age, you can maintain strength, vitality, and appearance through weight training and aerobics. Weight training enables you to maintain muscle mass in the proper areas, builds better posture, and leads to a leaner, healthier body with a smaller percentage of body fat. Lower body fat enables your body to burn calories at rest, consequently keeping your weight under control and creating greater self-esteem by knowing you look and feel great. I now have a higher level of energy and substantially greater stamina, which I attribute to being a vegetarian for the past seventeen years, as the following numbers suggest.

	AGE 30	AGE 47
Weight	192	168
Blood Pressure	140/100	96/62
Resting Heart Rate	72	59
Cholesterol	286	161
One Mile Run		6:35
Four Miles		31:00
Waist	35"	31"
Body Fat	18%	10%
Chest (expanded)		42"
Height	6'0"	6'0"
Bench Press		225 lb.

Vary your routine to keep your muscles off balance, which accelerates their growth: more reps, lighter weights; fewer reps, heavier weights. I engage in a full or light workout, depending on how my body feels.

Setting an Example

It is important that we set a good example for our children so that they will teach future generations the necessity for change. Copying the behavior of others has been one of the most common ways of learning for all of us and comes naturally to many animals. Learning through observation can certainly be an indication of intelligence. However, certain species are better at it than others.

The expression "copy cat" was coined, not by accident, but from the cat's ability to mimic actions of others. The best example of this is when a cat is stuck in a tree. Climbing up the tree becomes automatic, due to the design of the cat's claws, enabling them to climb in an upward motion. But descending from the tree, using those same claws isn't so easy. This activity is normally learned from the mother cat. However, it's not uncommon today for kittens to be separated from their mothers within six to eight weeks of birth, thus depriving the kitten of the opportunity to learn this behavior.

Similarly, dolphins have a strong tendency to mimic other dolphins. Trainers have observed that baby dolphins almost seem to learn simultaneously as the adult dolphins are trained to respond to different stimuli.

As humans, we generally use mimicry as a traditional teaching skill to learn everything from dancing, to swimming, to eating. Consider the impact advertising has on our society, and why so much money is spent to influence people. How often do overweight children have overweight parents, and overweight animals? My observation of a mother and her child eating breakfast one morning at a local restaurant proved that we are all conditioned. As they sat next to me, I watched the mother cut up her daughter's pancakes, sausage, and eggs and pour maple syrup on them. It occurred to me that this child was being conditioned by her mother what to expect for breakfast, what it will taste like, and how to prepare it. This experience could have just as easily included an alternate, completely healthy diet.

Our local cable company publishes the elementary school lunch program available for the week. The program recently included:

- Monday: Chicken Nuggets or Ham
- Tuesday: Taco or Hot Dog
- Wednesday: Cheese Pizza
- Thursday: Tuna Sandwich or Hamburger
- Friday :   Cheese and Ham Pita

This is what American school children are eating, not including their fast food diet after school. Some schools are even putting in food courts to provide a selection of various fast foods. The attitudes toward diet will also necessitate educating those responsible for teaching future generations, as well as altering the course of consumer likes and dislikes. Staying healthy requires more than good nutrition. Not smoking, working in a safe environment, getting regular check-ups, exercising, and wearing seat belts are all important preventative measures you can take to live a longer, happier, healthier life. Setting an example by following the guidelines below will help provide a more balanced diet.

- Eating a variety of foods
- Maintaining a desirable weight
- Avoiding too much saturated fat and cholesterol
- Eating foods with adequate starch and fiber
- Avoiding too much sugar and sodium
- Drink alcoholic beverages in moderation, or don't drink at all

The Times They Are A Changin'

Attitudes from generation to generation seem slow to change. However, as awareness becomes more prevalent, change does occur. For example, slowly changing awareness and attitudes toward wearing fur, purely for vanity's sake, is becoming a social liability. People are becoming increasingly aware of the mistreatment toward animals. I give a great deal of credit and respect to current fashion models Cindy Crawford and Christine Turlington in the U.S., and many others models in Europe for helping to increase this awareness. These women recently took a stand by saying they would rather go naked than wear fur. Also, the fur industry in Europe has nearly been eliminated by an aggressive, graphic ad campaign which affects consciousness and attitudes toward fur-wearing. This heightened sensibility, hopefully, will slowly start changing attitudes of future generations.

Traditions need to change sometimes for the betterment of a larger issue. Just because someone's great-grandfather did something, doesn't make it right or acceptable in today's society. The Gulf of Saint Lawrence seal hunt was finally banned in 1987 by the Canadian government only after international pressure was aroused from gruesome pictures which showed beautiful white seal pups being bludgeoned to death for their fur. The seal hunters were outraged that their cultural heritage, livelihood, and rights were being taken away. They have now come to realize that the revenue from tourism to see the seals in their natural habitat generates three times more money to them and their community than the hunting of the seal pups.

A World Bank study for Kenya showed that an average elephant herd generates about $610,000 a year in tourism income, which makes an individual elephant worth about $1 million over a sixty-year life span. Using elephant habitat for agriculture would return about $.33 per acre, but using it for grazing elephant herds to draw tourists generates about $17 per acre. As the

Kenyans say, "Wildlife pays, so wildlife stays"— and so does the Amboseli National Park to protect income-generated wildlife areas.

Summary

- Consult your physician.
- Purchase a good pair of athletic shoes.
- Stretch and warm up for about five minutes with some low level activity.
- Following the above guidelines, eventually work up to your target zone for twenty to forty minutes, three to five days per week.
- Always check your pulse rate during your activity to be careful not to exceed your maximum heart rate.
- Stay well hydrated by drinking plenty of water, before, during and after your workout.
- Follow your exercise routine with five minutes of cool down at a lower activity level.
- Finish with a few minutes of stretching.
- It's very important to find an exercise you like so you will continue it.
- Always listen to your body, if you experience any discomfort, stop and consult a physician (this is not a good time for denial).

All matters regarding you health require medical supervision. Consult your physician before starting a program, then find a good book on proper weight training, join a gym, or find a personal trainer that fits your situation. You can set an example by not settling for what's expected. The changes you make in your attitude and habits in eating and exercise can help you maintain proper nutrition, weight, and fitness. This lifestyle will help in preventing illness while living a longer, healthier, and more balanced life. Change is a natural part of growing and will help you in achieving a more meaningful life.

Chapter Six

Sharing Meaningful Relationships

*"A man is truly ethical only when he
obeys the compulsion to help all life
which he is able to assist, and shrinks
from injuring anything that lives."*
—Albert Schweitzer

This chapter explores how our diet affects our health, the economy, and the environment. Albert Schweitzer said, "Ultimately, a civilization will be judged on how it treats its animals." History is peppered with thousands of stories of animals performing near-miraculous, compassionate feats to save humans, as well as members of their own species, from harm.

The French Pass, the channel between the D'Urville Islands off New Zealand, offers a wonderful story of a selfless mammal named Pelorus Jack. This dangerous channel was notorious for its many jagged rocks and treacherous currents which, through the years, caused hundreds of shipwrecks. A dolphin named Pelorus Jack was first witnessed by crew members of the Boston schooner *Brendall* when he playfully appeared in the waters near their ship. Throughout his life, Pelorus Jack saved countless lives as he guided ships through this narrow channel. His guidance became so reliable, and ship's crews became so dependent on Pelorus Jack, they would actually wait at the entrance of the French Pass until the dolphin could safely escort them through the channel. However, on one occasion, while guiding a ship named The *Penguin*, a drunken passenger shot and wounded

Pelorus Jack. The passenger narrowly escaped with his life as the angry crew watched their dependable guide swim away, blood trailing from his wounded body. For several weeks, The *Penguin*, as well as all other ships, had to negotiate the treacherous rocks and currents of the channel without the help of their friend. Incredibly, the dolphin recovered and reappeared, obviously forgiving one human's cruel act and proceeded to guide ships through the channel once again. Thereafter, each time The *Penguin* entered the mouth of the channel, Pelorus Jack was nowhere to be found. The animal's seemingly endless commitment to escorting ships through the French Pass reportedly continued for many years, but the crew of The *Penguin* never saw him again. Tragically, some time later, The *Penguin* was shipwrecked during a storm traveling unguided through the channel. A significant number of passengers and crew were drowned.

The William O. Stillman award, given to pets who rescue their owners, was once given to Spud, a four year old Dalmatian, who successfully awakened his sleeping owner by biting his hand while a fire burned in the kitchen. After leaving the home, the owner called 911 as flames were reaching the kitchen ceiling, melting the microwave, and filling the house with smoke. Meanwhile, Spud had grabbed Gizmo, a five-month old kitten, by the scruff of the neck and taken her out of the house. This was the first time the Stillman Award had been awarded to a pet who, in addition to rescuing its owner, had also rescued another pet.

Unconditional Love

My loving wife, who I've been fortunate to share the past twenty-six years with, wrote the following to our friends after our golden retriever died several years ago:

"For the past sixteen years we were fortunate to share our hearts and our home with our golden retriever, Brie. We gave her shelter, we kept her safe, we kept her warm. She gave us her loyalty and devotion and showed us the true meaning of unconditional love. She was our constant companion and our very special friend. These past few years were truly a gift, one we found to be unbearable to give up. Our hearts never knew a greater joy, nor a more painful loss. Paul and I brought her home to live with us the first year of our marriage, she was five weeks old. She was so tiny that I put her in a shoe box to bring her home. She lived life to the fullest and stayed with us as long as she possibly could, until her frail little body couldn't fight any longer. The tiny shoe box has been replaced by a casket, she sleeps wrapped in her favorite blanket and still holds her little stuffed Santa pillow her 'Aunt Roz' made for her so many years ago. Brie is buried in her rock garden, the one she walked every day of her life. As fragile as her bones had become, and as tired as she must have been, she could not resist the allure of her magical, wonderful garden. Here is where she romped and played with the squirrels and birds, and made a special path winding though the bushes and trees. And here is where she now rests, her grave marked by a small stone angel sitting on a rock. She sleeps beneath the dogwood tree, and the squirrels she loved to taunt and chase now come to her, to bury their nuts and play above her. We always said, 'love us, love our dog,' as so many of you did. She was a little heartbreaker, even to the end. You have our love and our thanks for enjoying her with us in life, and sharing our grief at her death. Brie was a winter puppy, who absolutely loved the snow. We are thankful to God, who the morning after Brie's death, placed a fresh, white blanket of snow on her grave. We knew then that she was safe, and that God loves and protects us all."

These words, inspired by the loss of a companion we loved, certainly shows that animals play a very special part in our lives and in the world.

Reverence for Life

My wife gave me great comfort by telling me, "When we lose someone we love, we lose a piece of ourselves, and after we die we get all those pieces back." My only hope is that, as human beings, we can develop a greater reverence for all life. My wife and I have learned so much in life from our companionship with animals. Their unfailing and unquestionable devotion is something to be admired. This non-judgmental relationship between a person and an animal can bring a different meaning to the words respect, love, and unselfishness.

I have learned a great deal while training our current dog, Alex (affectionately nicknamed TWD "The Wonder Dog"). In many ways, immeasurable patience and understanding gave way to a lasting, deep respect for one another. This has taught me that there is always, ALWAYS, an alternative to a specific behavior. I have come to realize that, so often, the reaction we have to misbehavior on the part of our pets, children, spouses, or business associates cause us to react illogically. Our reactions are often the wrong ones. However, once you learn the proper method or behavior to correct a situation, the outcome can be very different, rewarding, and satisfying. I now marvel at watching other misbehaving dogs control their owners. There is a very simple solution to this other than jerking, yanking and yelling, or the worst of all, hitting. Behavior is a learned response which can be dealt with in a positive, constructive and reinforcing way, or in a very destructive way that destroys any bond that might have been created. This is true for animals as well as people. People often react rather than think. You have to slow your reaction time down or anticipate a situation where you think of the appropriate action in advance. Sometimes this simply requires being a little more creative than your child or dog. This should not be too difficult; therefore, why do we screw up so often? All it takes is to be just a little smarter than they are.

Largely, the most difficult part of training an animal is the handler or trainer knowing the right thing to do; or parents knowing the right thing to do when their children misbehave. This means doing something constructive rather than destructive. Instead of reinforcing bad behavior, you want to construct and create good behavior. As simple as this sounds, why is it that so many people lash out verbally or physically in an attempt to deal with or correct a behavior?

He Said, She Said

Two factors in any relationship which largely determine its success or failure may be the ability to communicate. You must also be unselfish. How do you know what someone is feeling, or how can you further deal with an issue, if you fail to communicate your concerns or problems? Also, if you deal with them in an unselfish way, by putting yourself in the other person's shoes, you may find what's in their best interest is also better for you. People often become what you expect them to become because they don't want to disappoint you. So if you continually strive to help or better the other person in your relationship, this can be a positive, constructive habit; and they will extend you the same courtesy. Reward people, give them your time.

Twenty-six years ago my wife and I made a pact that we would always try to compliment each other whether in private or in public. How often do you see couples nagging, or suggesting that their spouse or significant other comes up short or doesn't meet an expectation? This belittles the partner in the eyes of others. Consequently, they often pick up this negative habit and return the behavior. If you continually praise, constructively compliment, and tell others your spouse's positive points, your spouse will extend that same gesture to you. This builds a relationship based on a foundation of trust, mutual respect, and admiration. Emphasize each of your respective strong points rather than weaknesses. This reinforces positive behavior.

Two very important things in life are to be **understood** and to be **loved**. Lack of communication harbors anger, resentment, and frustration; all of which are destructive forces. Constructively and positively dealing with issues, coming to a solution (whatever that solution may be or however painful) is the best way to come to the right conclusion.

I'm OK, You're OK

The following methods of teaching and training clearly explain the fundamental principles of behavioral training through reinforcement. Here are eight methods to deal with habitual problems with your spouse, children, employees, family, or partner. These can be applied in any context of behavior.

1. Capital Punishment:
   This always works. It gets rid of the behavior by getting rid of the doer, temporarily or permanently. Method 1 solves the problem in a way but may or may not be the method of choice in any given situation.

   - Problem: Roommate leaves dirty laundry all over the place.
   - Solution: Change roommates.
   - Problem: Spouse habitually comes home in a bad mood.
   - Solution: Get divorced.

2. Punishment:
   These are seldom effective and lose effect with repetition but are widely used.

- Problem: Roommate leaves dirty laundry all over the place.
- Solution: Yell and scold. Threaten to confiscate and throw away the clothes, or do so.
- Problem: An adult offspring who you think should be self-sufficient wants to move back in with you.
- Solution: Let the adult child move in but make life miserable for him or her.

3. Negative Reinforcement:
   Negative reinforcement may be effective and the method of choice in some situations. The car device described here works very well, especially if the children are too tired and cross to be amenable to alternatives such as playing games and singing songs.

- Problem: Kids too noisy in the car.
- Solution: When decibel level meets the pain threshold, pull over and stop the car. Read a book. Ignore arguing about stopping; that's noise too. Drive on when silence reigns.
- Problem: An adult offspring who you think should be self-sufficient wants to move back in with you.
- Solution: Let adult child come back but charge him or her exactly what you would charge a stranger for rent, food, and any additional services such as laundry or baby-sitting. Make it worthwhile financially to move on.
- Problem: Spouse habitually comes home in a bad mood.
- Solution: Turn your back or leave room briefly when tone of his or her voice is disagreeable.

Return and give attention at once when voice is silent or normal.

4. Extinction:
Method 4 is not useful for getting rid of well learned, self-rewarding behavior patterns. It is good, however, for whining, sulking, or teasing. Even small children can learn—and are gratified to discover—that they can stop older children from teasing them merely by not reacting in any way, good or bad.

- Problem: Kids too noisy in the car.
- Solution: A certain amount of noise is natural and harmless; let it be, they'll get tired of it.
- Problem: An adult offspring who you think should be self-sufficient wants to move back in with you.
- Solution: Accept it as a temporary measure and expect that the adult child will move out as soon as finances improve or the present crisis is over.

5. Train an Incompatible Behavior:
Sensible people often employ this method. Singing and playing games in the car relieves parents as well as children from boredom. Diversion, distraction, and pleasant occupations are good alternatives during many tense moments.

- Problem: Spouse habitually comes home in a bad mood.
- Solution: Institute some pleasant activity on home-coming, incompatible with grouching, such as playing with the children, working on a

hobby. Thirty minutes of total privacy is often good. Spouse may need time to unwind before switching to family life.

6. Put the Behavior on Cue:
It doesn't seem logical that this method would work, but it can be startlingly effective, and sometimes almost an instantaneous cure.

- Problem: Roommate leaves dirty laundry all over the place.
- Solution: Have a laundry fight. See how big a mess you can both make in ten minutes. (Effective, Sometimes the untidy person, seeing what a big mess looks like, is then able to recognize and tidy up smaller messes—one shirt, two socks that may still bother you but were previously not perceived as messy by the roommate.)
- Problem: Spouse habitually comes home in a bad mood.
- Solution: Set a time and signal for grouching; sit down for ten minutes, say, starting at 5 p.m. During that period reinforce all complaining with your full attention and sympathy. Ignore complaining before and after.

7. Shape the Absence of Unwanted Behavior:
This takes some conscious effort over a period of time, but is often the best way to change deeply ingrained behavior.

- Problem: An adult offspring who you think should be self-sufficient wants to move back in with you.
- Solution: Reinforce adult children for living away from home when they are doing so. Don't criticize their housekeeping, choice of apartment, decor, or taste in friends, or they may decide you're right, your house is a better place to live

8. Change the Motivation:
   If you can find a way to do it, this method always works and is the best of all.

   - Problem: Roommate leaves dirty laundry all over the place.
   - Solution: Hire a maid or housekeeper to tidy up and do laundry, so neither you nor the roommate has to cope. This may be the best solution if you are married to this roommate and you both work. Or the messy person could shape the tidy one into being more casual.

These methods can be used to train your out-of-control dog, alter the behavior of misbehaving children, or change a relationship with an impossible teenager, negative parent or difficult spouse. Generally understanding these principles enables you to deal with problems and communicate more effectively. All this ensures a life with less conflict and a more loving and enjoyable overall environment. It is a reality in life that sooner or later your friends, associates, and family will disappoint you in some way or another. That just makes them human. Forgive them and get on with your life.

Child and Animal Abuse

Focusing behavior towards a greater reverence for all life presents another aspect of this picture. A major study at Yale University discovered a higher incidence of child animal abusers becoming violent criminals. Studies of inmates from several U.S. prisons found virtually none of these convicts had pets as children, and missed the opportunity to learn the value of life and living things. Many case histories bear this out.

- Albert DeSalvo, the Boston Strangler, who killed thirteen women in 1962-63, trapped dog and cats in orange crates and shot arrows through the boxes.
- Patrick Sherill, who killed fourteen co-workers in 1986 before killing himself, had no prior criminal record but had a history of animal abuse.
- New York's Son of Sam, David Berkowitz, who pled guilty to thirteen murder and attempted murder charges, had previously shot a neighbor's Labrador retriever.
- James Huberty, shot by police in 1984 after killing twenty-one children and adults at a California McDonald's, had been accused, as a teenager, of shooting his neighbor's dog with an air gun.

In some cases, the direct investigation of animal cruelty has led to the apprehension of violent criminals. However, these tendencies can, and have been, reversed—even in criminals. Research indicates that convicts who are given the opportunity to own a pet prior to their release show a much higher rate of success when readjusting to society. Owning a pet gave them something to love and care for, thereby giving them a purpose in life. This occurred in a penal system where released convicts are expected to be returned to jail more than 70 percent of the time.

As previously indicated, there are two fundamental needs of humans: to be understood and feel loved. This is further evidenced in the enormous success of companion animal programs instituted to complement the care of the elderly, the most rapidly growing segment of the U.S. population. Studies indicate these people, when given an animal, demonstrate a remarkable change in their attitude, thereby giving them a reason to care for themselves in the process.

> *"The greatness of a nation can be judged*
> *by how its animals are treated."*
> —Gandhi

Political Pollution

In order to connect a reverence for life to our health, the environment, and how our habits affect our lives, the following further explains. Studies encourage a shift toward a vegetarian diet rather than one in which five billion animals are killed annually. This, despite the fact that the American diet, traditionally high in animal fat, has been linked to cancer, heart disease, and osteoporosis.

> *"I have no doubt that it is part of*
> *the destiny of the human race and*
> *its gradual improvement to leave off*
> *eating animals."*
> — Henry David Thoreau

Official figures estimate several million dolphins which generally swim above salmon and tuna schools, called the Dall porpoise, have been killed in the past ten years by fishing methods using huge nets to trap salmon and tuna. This is done even though the Marine Mammal Protection Act of 1972 required a gradual decline to zero in the killing of porpoise. In 1981, the Reagan administration encouraged Congress to exempt the U.S. tuna fleet, permitting the continued use of purseseine nets which do not discriminate between the trapping and killing of thousands of dolphins with the intended tuna catch. In spite of the fishing industry's effort to convince the public that they have modified these nets to permit the dolphins an escape, these dolphins can still be caught and released so many times that they are battered , mangled, or drowned in the process. Using these nets are not as simple as trapping the intended tuna catch without also trapping and drowning seals, turtles, and birds. Every day fishing vessels worldwide comb the oceans leaving miles of plastic netting behind them which entangles and kills an estimated 100,000 marine mammals and at least one million birds annually. Factory farming ships virtually decimate the ocean floors when they drag their nets to capture their intended prey. They destroy coral beds, natural reefs, and subsequently discard any unwanted creatures through their portholes and back into the sea. This often leaves the creatures crippled, damaged, or dead. Fish are not the only species influenced by our diets. An even more profound effect is caused by the consumption of meat.

The "Beef" Bomb

There are 10,354,979 head of cattle in the United States according to the Census Bureau. Per day, they consume twenty pounds of grass and hay, forty gallons of water, and create ninety to 150 pounds of waste. For the record, that totals 207 million pounds of grass and hay, 414 million gallons of water, and 1.5 billion pounds of waste per day.

Worldwide, 650 million pigs are killed every year to produce 66 million tons of pork. The United States alone annually consumes 16 billion pounds of pork products. This is sad since pigs are incredibly affectionate, inquisitive, responsive, and brave animals. They have one of the highest measured IQs of all animals, even higher than the dog.

By cycling our grain supplies through livestock we end up with only 10 percent as many calories available for human consumption as would be available if we ate the grain directly. Less than half of the harvested agricultural land in the United States is used to grow food for people, the majority is used to grow livestock feed. This is a drastically inefficient use of our acreage. For every sixteen pounds of grain and soybeans used to feed beef cattle, we get back only one pound as meat on our plates. To supply one person with meat for a year requires three and one quarter acres of land. Supplying one pure vegetarian requires only one sixth of an acre. Therefore, a given acre can feed twenty times as many people eating a purely vegetarian diet, as it could those eating a standard meat-based diet. Lester Brown of the Overseas Development Council has estimated if Americans were to reduce their meat consumption by only 10 percent, it would free more than 12 million tons of grain annually for humans to eat. That by itself would be enough to adequately feed every one of the 60 million humans who will starve to death this year. By cycling grain through livestock, we waste 90 percent of its protein, 96 percent of its calories, 100 percent of its fiber, and 99 percent of its carbohydrates. According to Department of Agriculture statistics, one acre of land can grow 20,000 pounds of potatoes; the same acre of land, if used to grow cattle feed, produces less than 165 pounds of beef.

*"The time will come when men such as I
will look on the murder of animals as
they now look on the murder of men."*
— Leonardo DaVinci

As the popularity of U.S. meat-based diets gain recognition and emulation from developing Third World countries, these less-healthy countries will allocate an increasing percentage of their resources to meat production. This shift in dietary habits will likely increase the health care costs of these countries as it has in the U.S. About 75 percent of the Third World imports of barley, corn, sorghum, and oats are not fed to people but to animals. Consider these numbers:

- Amount of corn consumed by humans in the U.S.
  20 percent
- Amount of corn consumed by livestock
  80 percent
- Amount of soybeans consumed by humans
  10 percent
- Amount of soybeans consumed by livestock
  90 percent

A Shot in the Arm

Steroids and antibiotics are used excessively in disease prevention within the factory farming environment. This may have a long-term ill effect, for exposure to these substances may cause immunity to antibiotics in humans. Recent studies indicate that nearly 95 to 99 percent of all toxic residue in our diets comes from meat, fish, dairy products, and eggs. Experts in the New England Journal of Medicine cite that tuberculosis, staph, and pneumonia are on the rise. Antibiotics used in the food chain to stop disease among cattle, chicken, fish, and other animals enable germs to build resistance. A very real future risk exists that, over time, bacteria will develop antibiotic-resistant genes according to a Rockefeller University microbiology professor. Consider the following facts:

- Less than one out of every 250,000 slaughtered animals is tested for toxic chemical residue.
- The Atlanta Journal-Constitution published the results of interviews with eighty-four federal poultry inspectors from thirty-seven processing plants in the five states that produce over half of all American chicken. Sixty of the eight-four poultry inspectors interviewed said that based on what they observe they no longer eat chicken.

I Feel the Earth Move

If history repeats itself, there is much to be learned from many great civilizations that have been lost, including ancient Egypt, Greece, and the Mayans. A major factor in determining the decline and demise of these great civilizations may have involved soil erosion, as indicated by many archaeologists. In their book *Top Soil In Civilization*, Verman Carter and Tom Dale pointed out that wherever soil erosion has destroyed the fertility base on which civilizations have been built, these civilizations have perished. Nutrient-rich top soil is the very basic foundation of life which holds moisture, feeds our plants, and sustains life on Earth. We have already lost potentially 75 percent of this precious top soil over the past 200 years in America's crop lands. As a result, the U.S. Department of Agriculture says productivity of the nation's croplands is down 70 percent, with much of it on the brink of becoming barren wasteland. Agriculture techniques currently employed to produce massive amounts of livestock feed require unprecedented amounts of chemical fertilizers and pesticides. More than 20 million tons of chemical fertilizers are applied each year by American farmers in a process that continually poisons the environment and accelerates the loss of top soil. The great native American Chief Seattle wrote these compassionate words more than 100 years ago.

"Where is man without the beast? If the beast were gone, man would die from a great loneliness of spirit, for whatever happens to the beast, soon happens to man. All things are connected, this we know. The earth does not belong to man, man belongs to the earth, this we know, all things are connected like the blood which unites one family. All things are connected. Whatever befalls the earth befalls the son of the earth. Man did not weave the web of life, he is merely a strand in it. Whatever he does to the web, he does to himself..."

The Rain Forests

In the continuing effort to supply America with a beef-oriented diet, plus the relentless pressure to produce higher yields from the land, we have lost hundred of millions of acres to soil erosion. This has set the stage for another devastating scenario: destroying our forests to provide more grazing land. One hundred years ago, 34 percent of the earth's land was covered by forests, today only 26 percent is covered.

Approximately 260 million acres of forest in the United States has been converted to supply the eating habits of most Americans. At this present pace of deforestation, in fifty years, the United States could be completely stripped of all its forests. It is estimated that nearly 200 million of these acres could be converted to forest if we stopped producing food to feed livestock and, instead, used the remaining land to produce food to feed people directly. A further exacerbation of this problem is found in

Central America in the devastation currently underway in the rain forests, mostly for the purpose of producing cheap beef.

Cattle ranching has destroyed more rain forests in Central America than any other single activity. According to a recent report issued by The World Watch Institute, the cost of a hamburger produced on former jungle land turned into pasture for grazing would be about $200. This allows for species loss, flood damage, erosion, and change of climate.

> *"Most people are largely unaware of the wide-ranging effect cattle are having on the ecosystems of the planet and the fortunes of civilization. Yet, cattle production and beef consumption now rank among the greatest threats to the future well being of the Earth and its human population."*
> —Jeremy Rifkin

It is estimated that during the past twenty-five years the amount of virgin rain forest in Central America has declined from 130,000 square miles to less than 80,000. If this pace were to continue, the entire tropical rain forest could disappear in another forty years. There are also more far-reaching effects. While these forests represent only 30 percent of the world's rain forests, they contain 80 percent of the world's vegetation, a substantial amount of the world's oxygen supply, and provide homes to half the species inhabiting the world we all share. More nutrients are stored in the trees of tropical rain forests than plants in northern forests. Consequently, as the tropical rain forests are destroyed for grazing land, the soil becomes less rich and contains fewer nutrients. It takes two and one half acres of land to support one steer. Clearing the land for grazing causes an acceleration of soil erosion by heavy rains. Through this continuing erosion process, in a few short years, the same steer requires twelve acres. Within ten years, that steer may require as much as twenty acres. Native people in these regions suffer the worst consequences. As more land is used to produce food for cattle, the price of this food increases, and starvation is often the result. Environmentally, this process causes more flooding. Entire tribal populations are being dislocated and becoming extinct from the environmental destruction this process precipitates. In turn, this accelerates the continuing loss of many migrating birds, which proportionately increases the population of insects which then necessitates an increase in pesticide use. All these factors hasten species extinction.

The destruction of these habitats in the tropics may ultimately cause the extinction of more than one million species within the next thirty years. What if it is found that one-quarter of the raw materials in these forests could provide the necessary ingredients for new medicines? Elimination of these forests may mean that we may never know what illnesses could have been cured.

The process of species extinction is much the same as popping rivets from the wing of a giant aircraft. One, two, even three or more of these, in the short run, may not cause a problem. The question ultimately becomes: How many lost rivets will it take to compromise the integrity of the aircraft's ability to fly, ultimately causing its destruction?

The Drink of Life

We take water for granted. Yet, as entire industries are formed to provide bottled water, it makes us pause to consider the future consequences of continuing the paths we now walk. We can buy distilled water, but what are the birds, deer and all other life forms to drink? Many warning signs can be directly related to the worldwide production and consumption of beef. Over half of the water consumed in the United States is used for the growing of feed for livestock (e.g. irrigation). An average of 2.5 thousand gallons of water are required to produce a single pound of meat. A month's household water supply, typically more than four thousand gallons, is required to produce a day's food for a meat eater. Compare this to only three hundred gallons needed for a pure vegetarian diet. More than 100 times more water is needed to produce a pound of meat than to a pound of vegetable product. *Newsweek* magazine summed up this situation when it said: "The water that goes into a thousand pound steer would float a destroyer."

One of California's leading environmental problems is lack of water. Think about that while you consider the following water amounts needed to produce one edible pound of food in that state:

- Lettuce - 23 gallons
- Potatoes - 24 gallons
- Apples - 49 gallons
- Chicken - 815 gallons
- Pork - 1,630 gallons
- Beef - 5,214 gallons

Cornell economist David Fields studied the fiscal consequences of water subsidies to the meat industry: "Reports by the General Accounting Office, the Rand Corporation and the Water Resources Council, have made it clear that irrigation and water subsidies to livestock producers are economically counter-productive. Every dollar state governments dole out to livestock producers in the form of irrigation subsidies, actually cost taxpayers more than seven dollars in lost wages, higher living costs, and reduced business income. The seventeen western states receive limited precipitation; yet their water supplies could support an economy and population twice the size of their present ones, but most of the water goes to produce livestock, directly or indirectly. Thus, current water use practices now threaten to undermine the economies of every state in the region."

The high plains region of Kansas, Colorado, Oklahoma, Nebraska and New Mexico produce half the nation's grain-fed beef. To produce the majority of this beef, water must be obtained from the great Ogallala Aquifer. The Ogallala Aquifer remained virtually untapped until fifty years ago. Now, demand for water from the Ogallala exceeds 13 trillion gallons every year. The amount of water withdrawn for the Ogallala Aquifer today is far more than what would be needed to grow the entire fruit and vegetable crop in the United States. What took millions of years to form is now being depleted at any alarming rate. We seem to be increasingly on a collision course with dangerous habits, traditions, and ways of life. We need to recognize that change is necessary to secure that we, and future generations, will continue to enjoy the wonderful natural resources of this planet.

The fact that the longer-term availability of water may be compromised is only one reason the American diet needs to change. As this natural resource is depleted, the quality of our water supply becomes more and more contaminated. The removal of manure from livestock feeding areas ultimately finds its way into the ground water and, eventually, into wells and public water systems. The amount of fecal matter produced from livestock raised for meat and dairy products produces approximately 340 billion pounds of waste each year. U.S. livestock produce twenty times as much excrement as the country's entire human population. The largest feed lots consisting of 100,000 cattle produces a waste problem equal to many American cities. Without adequate water supplies, the world will not be able to support future population growth.

Condom Sense?

The population of the world now exceeds 6 billion. However, it is estimated that only 1 billion live above the poverty level and approximately 40,000 children die each day of malnutrition. The fact is that the United States represents only 5 percent of the world's population, yet we consume 25 percent of its natural resources. The massive consumption by this nation creates virtually half the garbage on this planet.

Twenty-one percent of the world's population (more than 1.2 billion people) live in China, a third world nation with a changing culture and economy. These people are currently entering the information age and developing appetites for Western technology and products, as well as Western meat-based diets. Adopting this diet puts further burdens on their economic and agricultural systems in an effort to produce the needed food.

Since the late 1960s when the USA and the United Nations began funding population programs, great progress has been made in many countries like Thailand, India, and Latin America in reducing birth rates. In the developed world population, growth has slowed to near zero in countries like Spain, Japan, Germany, and the U.S. This progress has, however, not been effective in Africa and other parts of the world. The United Nations estimate of the world population in 2050 may be 12.5 billion, over twice the world population today. It took 123 years for the world population to grow from 1 billion to 2 billion, but only thirteen years to grow from 4 billion to 5 billion. These numbers cannot be supported by a meat-based diet. Reducing population growth is infinitely complex and a completely different issue. However, I feel whatever forms of family planning are adopted, it will surely be easier to feed the world on a meatless diet. In our century, Gandhi urged people to live simply so others might simply live. Also, Nobel Prize winner Henry Kendall of the Union of Concerned Scientists said, "If we do not stabilize population with justice, humanity and mercy... it will be done for us by nature, and it will be done brutally." On the surface, it may seem that a dietary shift in this country would not be able to impact all these circumstances. It clearly has to be far more complex than this, but is it? These effects cause consequences that create hunger and starvation as well as economic and political conflict throughout the world.

Summary

For every billion burgers sold, another hundred species become extinct from the tropical rain forests which could make a difference in the treatment or cure for AIDS. The continued use of chemicals in this vicious cycle of producing greater yields undermines our natural resources. Lands that experience greater top soil erosion could precipitate the elimination of forests, increase air and water pollution, and contribute to global warming. From a nation that has so much, maybe much more should be expected. The U.S. has and can take a leading role, setting an example for the world's developing countries, and future generations who emulate what we do as a model on which to build their future.

We can become a healthier and more sensitive society by realizing that change creates opportunity. This is indeed an opportunity for all of us to consciously strive to make a difference.

Lower health care costs, a greater reverence for all life, and a better environment can be achieved through a fundamental change in dietary habits. A better balance in all these areas will provide a more productive and brighter future not only for us but for future generations to come.

Chapter Seven

The Best Is Yet to Come

*"One man can completely change the
character of his country and the
industry of its people by dropping a
single seed in the soil."*
—John C. Gifford

C hange consists of taking a step in the right direction, one small step at a time toward your ultimate goal. We live in a world that provides more opportunities for us than any prior generation in history. It is up to us to recognize and make the necessary changes for a more balanced life. We have seen democracy prevail around the world, and watched as other countries emulate the United States. It has been said that democracy is the worst form of government, except for all the others that have been tried from time to time. So with all democracy's faults and frailties, it is still the finest system on the face of the earth. As proof of our system prevailing throughout the world, we witnessed the dismantle of the Berlin Wall, the world wide collapse of Communism, and the development of the European Economic Community which removed trade barriers that have been in place in excess of 500 years.

Common Cents

The world already shares a common currency and language: electronics and English. Peter T. White, writing in the *National Geographic* magazine, gives us a personal illustration of electronic currency. "I'm in Paris, it's late evening, and I need money, quickly. The bank I go to is closed, of course, but outside sits an ATM, an automated teller machine—and look what can be made to happen, thanks to computers and high-speed telecommunications. I insert my ATM card from my bank in Washington, DC, and punch in my identification number and the amount of 1,500 francs, roughly equivalent to $300. The French bank's computers detect that it's not their card, so my request goes to the Cirrus system's inter-European switching center in Belgium, which detects that it's not a European card. The electronic message is then transmitted to the global switching center in Detroit, which recognizes that it's from my bank in Washington. The request goes there, and my bank verifies that there's more than $300 in my account and deducts $300 plus a $1.50 fee. Then it's back to Detroit, to Belgium, and to the Paris bank and its ATM—and out comes $300 in French francs. Total elapsed time: sixteen seconds."

Fasten Your Seat Belt

The end of the Cold War provided us with an opportunity to live in a safer world and taught us to learn to deal more responsibly with nuclear weapons. Incredible advancements in medicine enable us to live longer, healthier lives. The explosion of telecommunications enables the communities of the world to become kindred in creating a larger picture of economic opportunity, prosperity, and consciousness to the environment, human rights, and business ethics. In the midst of this wonderful progress, there still remains far too much imbalance in the world. The consequences of this are seen every day in the growing numbers of the poor, the loss of natural resources, and the escalation of violent crime, which is not only perpetrated on adults, but also on children by children. Only half of this country's children under the age of eighteen live with both their parents, which is caused by an increasing erosion of family values.

The fiscal irresponsibility of the government, not cutting wasteful expenses, and better allocating tax revenues to support the economy continues to perpetuate these inequities. One of the places revenue needs to be re-allocated is to foreign countries. The answer is not always just aid or assistance, though necessary in times of crisis. It is important to teach the skills and provide the tools so these countries can become independent and learn to feed themselves. These imbalances can be corrected and changed.

Change, now more than ever, is necessary not only for the survival of this world, but for its improvement. We must protect our natural resources, provide necessary services for world communities, and strive to live in a truly global society, overcoming the discrimination that has existed for too many generations. We have to start by changing ourselves for the better, which, in turn, will inspire others to change. Our actions not only affect our lives, but all those we associate with as we strive to be an example for others. One penny, if doubled every day becomes $21,474,836 in one month. One person fostering change soon becomes two, then a group and ultimately a majority.

Life is not a dress rehearsal—you only get one take. The business of living the best life you can, one day at a time, has an almost unbelievable cumulative effect for good success and for achieving the things you want. It's important to understand that "the true worth of a man may be measured by the objects he refuses to pursue or acquire," Chinese proverb. The greatest blessings in life are already within you.

Pony Express to E-Mail

As a nation we have progressed from an agrarian society to the Industrial Revolution that forces the American worker to retire at age sixty-five. The fact is, physical labor becomes increasingly more difficult for those over age sixty-five. This perception has continued into the information and technologically advanced society in which we now live. The irony of this progress is that the elderly are our largest growing population segment, and as the baby boomers join this formidable group, the old perception of retiring at sixty-five no longer applies. This growing group of talented, resourceful, and experienced individuals may live twenty to thirty years beyond age sixty-five and need to continue living productive lives to maintain the self-esteem they worked so long and hard to develop. The only way we can provide this productive environment is through continued learning.

Japanese children attend school eight hours per day, 240 days per year, resulting in only half of one percent of Japanese children being functionally illiterate. American children attend school six hours per day, 180 days per year, with a deplorable eight percent of our seventeen-year-olds being functionally illiterate.

Today's younger computer literate generations place the older population at a distinct disadvantage. To capture the attention of the younger generation who were weaned in this environment, it is necessary for all those who are not computer knowledgeable to become familiar with this technology. Understanding this area is essential to the older generation in order to remain competitive and stay ahead of the learning curve. I encourage all ages to become computer literate if you want to remain a rival in a world continually more dependent on this technology. Computers give everyone the ability to be competitive and are a wonderful way to learn any subject or area of interest. They give everyone the opportunity to continue to grow in a world that is constantly changing, and may require you to change professions as obsolescence often gets in the way of progress. Another major benefit of a computer in the home is that children who use them tend to watch less television. The average child age two to twelve watches nearly thirty-two hours of television per week.

To dramatize this process, consider that today's 486 computer chip can scan the Encyclopedia Britannica—all twenty-nine volumes of 29,000 + pages—and select a single bit of information in two seconds. Intel's 8088 chip, introduced in 1981 as part of IBM's first PC, took five minutes. The newest entry in computer chips, Pentium, is five times faster than its predecessor, the 486.

William Gates, president of Microsoft, became a billionaire and one of American's wealthiest individuals. His ingenuity and recognition that the computer industry would give mainstream America the ability to learn and use computers easily through a "Windows" (as opposed to DOS) environment made computers accessible to everyone with the click of a mouse. His foresight made him a rich man.

"Windows" is becoming the standard environment for the PC industry. It enables a larger number of people to use computers more easily. An increasing number of people, for at least part of their business day, work at home via computer modem. This group has grown from 3 million people in 1989 to 7.6 million in 1993 and likely to continue.

"A" Is for Attitude

The most important factor in guaranteeing exceptional results in life is attitude. More than anything else, your attitude at the beginning of a difficult task will determine its success or failure. Your attitude toward others determines their approach toward you. Look for the best in people and their ideas; don't waste time talking about your problems. Stop making excuses; instead, adopt a spirit of well-being and confidence. Treat everyone with whom you come in contact as an important person. Our physical environment and the world in which we live and work are the mirrors of our disposition and our expectations. Life is a state of mind. We are what we think, whom we associate with, and what we eat. There is nothing in the world more worth striving for than self-esteem. If we feel we are important, recognized, needed and respected, we will give our love and respect to the person who most fills those needs. Look around you and realize that, at this moment, you are a living example of the sum total of your thoughts. At this point in your life, if you don't like what you see, change it. There are now more opportunities before you than at any other time in history.

The Miracle of Life

No one can take your place. To be what you are and to realize what you are capable of becoming is the secret to a happy life. Successful people have a desire to succeed despite any handicap. In addition, by envisioning exactly what they want to do, they can overcome every obstacle. Hold on tight and embrace your dreams with courage, persistence, and compassion. You can have what you want, you only need to make up your mind. Pursue your goals with unfailing honesty and integrity. Success is the progressive realization of a worthy goal. Always remember that nothing can take the place of persistence and determination. Do the very best in the things that you do, and the very best is what you will be.

> *"It is not so important to be serious,*
> *as it is to be serious*
> *about the important things."*
> —Robert Maynard Hutchins

Together we inhabit this tiny planet. This was acutely brought to our attention when the space program began launching satellites enabling us to view this wonderful planet from 150 miles above the earth. It was then that we saw how really small the Earth is. It helped us realize we all breathe the same air, drink the same water, and have within ourselves the responsibility to coexist with this fragile world and its natural resources. Doing the right things today will allow us to leave this wonderful experience we call "life" as a legacy for future generations. Life holds so many miracles. Stop for a moment and you'll realize it requires a continuing, conscious effort to hold dear all those things in life that are important to you and pursue them with passion. So celebrate your successes, keep a good sense of humor, don't take yourself too seriously, shake off your failures. Turn up the music. It can lift your spirits, soothe your soul, clear your mind, bring a tear to your eye, and a smile to your face.

You can make a difference, one small step at a time by always trying to do the right thing. These are the qualities to achieve a more balanced, productive, and fulfilled life.

- Persistence
- Enthusiasm
- Accountability
- Passion
- Honesty
- Integrity
- Discipline
- Communication

- Unselfishness
- Attitude
- Optimism

If you build the foundation of your life and career around these qualities and include the habits and discipline of the other aspects of this book you can achieve your most challenging goals for love, health, happiness, and wealth. This is a way of life, a lifestyle with uncompromising integrity. May you exceed your most daring dreams and be the best you can be. Tomorrow is a new beginning. Take a deep breath and jump into the rest of your life.

Notes

Chapter One

Recognizing a Need for Change

2 The U.S. Census Bureau, number of households and net worth statistics in the United States. Congressional Budget Office, three percent statistic.

Margaret L. Usdansky, poverty line, "More Suburban Kids Living in Poverty," *USA TODAY*, Copyright September 27, 1994. Reprinted with permission.

4 U.S. Department of Commerce Economics and Statistics Administration, and the Bureau of the Census 1992, medium income.

Anne R. Carey and Marcy E. Mullins, personal exemptions, "Shrinking Tax Breaks," *USA TODAY*, Copyright 1993. Reprinted with permission. Source: James Steele and Donald Bartlett, *America: Who Really Pays the Taxes?*

5 Phil Hampton, "Sales Swell after Luxury Tax Drowns." *USA TODAY*, Copyright 1993. Reprinted with permission.

6 Yankelovich Partners Inc., poll statistics. *Time/CNN*, 1994, p. 49. Reprinted with permission.

12 The National Association of Security Dealers, licensed representative statistics.

Steve Lewis, "True Confessions," Reprinted with permission *Barron's*, © 1989 Dow Jones & Company, Inc.

13 The American Bar Association Research Department, statistics on lawyers.

Chapter Two
Positioning Yourself to Succeed

17   Kent Mangelson, research on professional status.

19-20   Ibid., consumer retention.

20-21   Ibid., specialization.

23-25   Ibid., income allocation.

27-29   Al Weis and Jack Trout, "Six Horses To Ride." *Positioning the Battle for your Mind* © 1983. Reprinted with permission of McGraw-Hill, Inc.
Malcolm S. Forbes, Sr., quotes, *"The Further Sayings of Chairman Malcolm."* Reprinted by permission of FORBES Magazine © Forbes, Inc.

Chapter Three
The People Mover

34-36   Sam Walton, *Ten Rules of Success*. Reprinted with permission of WAL★MART.

Chapter Four
Managing Your Finances

45   Leslie Wayne, American home owners invest in mutual funds... "Generation of Savers Now Turns to Investing," *The New York Times*, Copyright 1993. Reprinted with permission.

50-54   Phil Carret, *Wall Street Week With Louis Rukeyser*, #711 "Wall Street Pioneer," September 9, 1977. Excerpted with permission of *Wall Street Week*.

55-56   Thomas Jaffe, "A Talk with John Templeton." Excerpted by permission of FORBES Magazine © Forbes Inc., 1988.

59   Daniel Kadlec, C.D. net return after inflation, "Professor: History Favors Stock Market," August 19, 1994. *USA TODAY*, Copyright 1994. Reprinted with permission.

59-60 Federal Reserve Board, CPI, "What has been the real return after inflation on a C.D.?"

66 Lewin/ICF, Life-Savings of the Average Fifty Year-Old.

68 James R. Healey, "Nostalgia Fuels Mustang Fever," November 22, 1993. Copyright 1993, *USA TODAY*. Reprinted with permission.

73 University of Michigan, study, "The Penalty for Missing the Market."
    Market timer studies, *The Idex Investment Advantage*, Vol. 3, issue 4, 1993. Reprinted with permission.
    Ibid., "What is the Difference Between Investing at Market High and Low?" Vol. 3, Issue 4, 1993.

74 Donald Cudney, InterSecurities, Inc. "The Wall Street Waltz," September 1991. Reprinted with permission.

75 Kadlec, "Professor: History Favors Stock Market," August 19, 1994.
    Daniel Kadlec, Nikkei declines, "Japanese Stocks: Bargains or Bums?" January 28, 1994. *USA TODAY*, Copyright 1994. Reprinted with permission.

79 Morgan Stanley Capital International World Index, stock market capitalization 1973 and 1993, Pioneer Funds Distributor, Inc., 2003 statistic.
    Morgan Stanley, China/USA television comparison, *Asia Week*.

Chapter Five
Fit for Life

83 John Robbins, medical schools, *May All Be Fed: Diet For A New World*. Copyright 1992. By permission of William Morrow & Company, Inc.
    Mike Snieder, Yale-Harvard alumni study, "Leaner Men Live Longer, Healthier," December 15, 1993. Copyright 1993, *USA TODAY*. Reprinted with permission.

American Medical Association Journal, U.S. population overweight.

84 Deidre Schwiesow and Marty Baumann, "50 Million Americans Spend $32 Billion Dieting," *USA TODAY*, Copyright 1994. Reprinted with permission.
Jennifer Chrebet, "Pulsepoint: Adolescent Obesity is not only a health hazard..." *American Health* © 1993. Researchers at Harvard University and New England Medical Center, Boston.

85 Billy Ray Boyd, Vegetarianism, *For The Vegetarian in You*, Taterhill Press, San Francisco, p. 17.

86 The American Heart Association and National Cancer Institute, "Recommended Caloric Intake from Fat."

96 AT&T Documentary, coronary heart disease, "A Part of your Life: My Heart, Your Heart."

97 Duke University Medical Center and the American Heart Association, national treatment costs.
AT&T Documentary, largest portion of health care costs.
Tim Friend, federal sponsored study. "Stroke: Among Most Costly Health Woe's," *USA TODAY*, Copyright 1994. Reprinted with permission.
Tim Friend, heart and blood vessel disease statistic, "Kids Smoking, Head Start on Heart Ailments," *USA TODAY*, Copyright 1994. Reprinted with permission.
Url Ubell, $50 billion spent on coronary care, "When is Heart Surgery Really Called For?" *Parade*, March 13, 1994.

98 Michael Turk, menopause and stroke statements, "Perception vs. Reality," *American Health*, December 1993, p. 57. Reprinted with permission.

100 National Academy of Sciences, correlation between dietary fat and the occurrence of cancer.

American Cancer Institute, news about cancer prevention.

American Cancer Foundation, high cholesterol diet increase chances of lung cancer.

Kenneth J. Pienta and Peggy S. Esper, study of dietary fat and risk of prostate cancer, "Is Dietary Fat a Risk For Prostate Cancer?" Journal of the National Cancer Institute, Vol. 85, No. 19, October 6, 1993.

Lorelei DiSogra, Ed. D., R. D., Diet, *Nutrition, and Cancer Prevention: A Guide to Food Choices*. Adapted from *Nutrition and Cancer Prevention*.

Robbins, Dr. Walden Bello, Executive Director, "American fast food diets...," Institute for Food and Development Policy, p. 255.

101 Editors of *Men's Health*, Harvard alumni study, p. 21, *How Men Stay Young*, Copyright 1991. Reprinted with permission by Rodale Press, Inc.

103 Robbins, female bone loss, *May All Be Fed: Diet for a New World*, p. 272.

105 Karen Pryor, copying the behavior of others, *Don't Shoot the Dog*, Copyright © 1983. Reprinted with permission of Simon & Schuster, Inc.

107 John Naisbitt, world bank study and the St. Lawrence seal hunt, *Global Paradox*, Copyright © 1994, p. 129. By permission of William Morrow & Company, Inc.

Chapter Six
Sharing Meaningful Relationships

111 John Robbins, animals performing miraculous feats. Excerpted with permission from *Diet For A New America*. (Published by Stillpoint Publishing, Walpole NH, 800-847-4014.)

112   Donna Berkelhammer, The William Stillman Award, "Life Saving Dog Given National Honor," *The Harold*, November 21, 1991.

116-120   Pryor, eight methods to change behavior, *Don't Shoot the Dog*, p. 107,108.

121   Robbins, Dr. Steven Kellert, refocusing behavior, Yale University, p. 23.

"Animal Cruelty: No Small Matter," *Police Journal: News Briefs*, p. 14, July 1987.

Ibid., "Apprehension of Violent Criminals."

George Washington School of Medicine, *American Health*, Copyright © March 1989. Reprinted with permission.

122-123   Robbins, "Dall Porpoise," *Diet for a New America*, p. 31.

123   Government Census Bureau, the number of cattle in the United States.

124   Robbins, cycling our grain, *Diet for a New America*, p. 351.

125   Consumption of natural resources, *American Health*, March 1989. Reprinted with permission.

World Watch Institute, third world imports, "Taking Stock: Animal Farming and the Environment." Reprinted with permission.

Doug Levy, steroids and antibiotics, "Overuse of Antibiotics Real Threat," April 28, 1994. *USA TODAY*, Copyright 1994. Reprinted with permission.

Robbins, toxic residue study, *Diet for a New America, p. 315.*

126   *Scott Bronstin, poultry inspector quote. "Chicken; How Safe?"* The Atlanta Journal Constitution, May 26, 1991. Reprinted with permission.

Robbins, great civilizations, *Diet for a New America*, p. 356.

Robbins, chemical fertilizers and pesticides, *Diet for a New America*, p. 357.

127 Steve Lustgarden, earth's land, "Teetering on a Limb," *Vegetarian Times*, April 1994, p. 17. Reprinted with permission.

128 Robbins, Distruction of habitats and water consumption in the U.S., *Diet for a New America*, p. 367.
Ibid., U.S. forests, *Diet for a New America*, p. 362, 363.

130 David Fields and Robin Hier, water subsidies. Reports by the General Accounting Office, Derand Corporation and the Water Resources Council, p. 367, 368.

132 Eileen Glanton, population growth statistics, "World Population Conference," *The Oakland Press*, September 5, 1994. Copyright permission granted by Associated Press.
Margaret L. Usdanski, Nobel Prize winner Henry Kendall, "Population Growing at a Furious Rate." *USA TODAY*, Copyright 1994. Reprinted with permission.

133 Lustgarden, cost of a hamburger, "Teetering on a Limb."

Chapter Seven

The Best Is Yet to Come

136 Peter T. White, "The Power of Money," National Geographic, January 1993. Reprinted with permission.

137 Margaret L. Usdansky, half of USA's children, "More Kids Live in Changing Families," August 30, 1994. *USA TODAY*, Copyright 1994. Reprinted with permission.

139 Kathy Rebello, 486 computer chip, "Super-Chip puts Mainframe on Desktop," December 9, 1988. *USA TODAY*, Copyright 1988. Reprinted with permission.
Patti Stang and Cliff Vancura, "Commuting Without Moving," *USA TODAY*, Copyright 1993. Reprinted with permission.

*"We make a living by what we get, we
make a life by what we give"*
—Winston Churchill

Index

About the Author

Paul H. Heneks is a career broker of twenty-three years and is currently a Registered Principal and Registered Investment Advisor Representative of InterSecurities, Inc., member NASD, SIPC, and SEC Registered Investment Advisor. He specializes in brokering professional money management, involving transactions totaling in excess of $500 million in securities, through retail and wholesale activities. Paul frequently lectures to colleges, organizations and corporations.